Reshaping Defence Diplomacy: New Roles for Military Cooperation and Assistance

Andrew Cottey and Anthony Forster

ADELPHI PAPER 365

Oxford University Press, Great Clarendon Street, Oxford OX2 6DP
Oxford New York

Athens Auckland Bangkok Bombay Calcutta Cape Town
Dar es Salaam Delhi Florence Hong Kong Istanbul Karachi
Kuala Lumpur Madras Madrid Melbourne Mexico City Nairobi
Paris Taipei Tokyo Toronto
and associated companies in Ibadan

Oxford is a trade mark of Oxford University Press

Published in the United States
by Oxford University Press Inc., New York

© The International Institute for Strategic Studies 2004

First published April 2004 by **Oxford University Press** for
The International Institute for Strategic Studies
Arundel House, 13–15 Arundel Street, Temple Place, London WC2R 3DX
www.iiss.org

Director John Chipman
Editor Tim Huxley
Copy Editor Matthew Foley
Production Simon Nevitt

British Library Cataloguing in Publication Data
Data available
Front cover: James V. Downen Jr., US Department of Defense

Library of Congress Cataloguing in Publication Data

ISBN 0-19-856653-0
ISSN 0567-932x

Contents

Tables

Introduction

Since the 1990s armed forces and defence ministries have taken on a growing range of peacetime cooperative tasks. In Europe, NATO's longstanding Western members now hold defence exercises alongside their former enemies from Eastern Europe, and provide assistance to these states in reforming their militaries. In Asia, the US has developed new military cooperation relationships with China and India, while a security dialogue has been initiated within the Association of South East Nations (ASEAN). In the Americas, Organisation of American States (OAS) defence ministers have met a number of times; Latin American states have established new bilateral defence ties; and longstanding military relations between the US and its southern neighbours have been redirected towards new goals. In Africa, Western governments are supporting countries in reforming their armed forces and developing indigenous peacekeeping capabilities, while the African Union (as the Organisation of African Unity was renamed in 2002) and subregional groups such as the Southern African Development Community (SADC) have established multilateral defence cooperation processes. In post-conflict countries such as Mozambique, Sierra Leone and Afghanistan, external powers are assisting governments' efforts to rebuild and reform their armed forces. Taken together, these activities represent a significant shift in patterns of peacetime international military cooperation.

The concept of defence diplomacy encapsulates this shift. The role of armed forces has traditionally been defined by the functional imperative of the use or threat of force – whether for purposes of defence, deterrence, compellance or intervention. Defence diplomacy, in contrast, involves the peacetime cooperative use of armed forces and related infrastructure (primarily defence ministries) as a tool of foreign and security policy. Over the last decade, there has been a growing trend, especially amongst the Western democracies, towards the use of defence ministries and armed forces as means of building cooperative relations with other states, and supporting other states in reforming their militaries. Western militaries are thus tasked not only with the more traditional role of preparing for and undertaking the use of force, but increasingly also with the new defence diplomacy role of peacetime cooperative engagement with other states. This involves not only longstanding cooperation arrangements amongst allies, but also cooperation with new partners and engagement with states undergoing difficult democratic and post-conflict transitions.

Defence diplomacy encompasses a wide range of activities that might in the past have been described as military cooperation or military assistance (see Table 1). Few of these activities are in themselves new. The practice of appointing defence attaches emerged as part of nineteenth-century European diplomacy.[1] Multinational military cooperation amongst European states can be traced back even earlier, and has been a common part of intra-alliance behaviour in the modern European state system. The European imperial powers developed close military relations with their colonies. The UK established the Imperial Defence College in 1922 to train senior military officers from, and develop a common military doctrine in defence of, the British Empire. In France, the Ecole Supérieur de Guerre served a similar function. As decolonisation proceeded after the Second World War, many former colonies chose to maintain extensive military links to their former colonial powers, especially Britain and France. During the Cold War, the US and the Soviet Union developed military ties with their respective allies around the world, providing arms, military training and other forms of assistance, and engaging in extensive bilateral and multilateral defence cooperation. Much activity that might be described as defence diplomacy was common practice within NATO, the Warsaw Pact and other alliance relationships for decades.

Since the 1990s, however, there has been an important shift in the nature and purposes of international military cooperation, especially for the Western democracies. Historically, military cooperation and assistance have largely been part of international realpolitik, balance-of-

Table 1: **Defence diplomacy activities**
• Bilateral and multilateral contacts between senior military and civilian defence officials.
• Appointment of defence attaches to foreign countries.
• Bilateral defence cooperation agreements.
• Training of foreign military and civilian defence personnel.
• Provision of expertise and advice on the democratic control of armed forces, defence management and military technical areas.
• Contacts and exchanges between military personnel and units, and ship visits.
• Placement of military or civilian personnel in partner countries' defence ministries or armed forces.
• Deployment of training teams.
• Provision of military equipment and other material aid.
• Bilateral or multilateral military exercises for training purposes.

power politics and the pursuit of narrowly-defined national interests. States engaged in defence cooperation with, and provided military assistance to, other states in order to counterbalance or deter enemies, maintain spheres of influence, support friendly regimes in suppressing domestic opponents or promote commercial interests (such as arms sales or more general trade relations). Military cooperation between the European imperial powers and their colonies reflected this logic, and the Cold War reinforced it. From a Western and especially US perspective, the strategic priority given to countering the Soviet Union and communism resulted in military cooperation with authoritarian regimes in many parts of the world.

The key shift of the last decade is that defence cooperation is now being used not only in its longstanding realpolitik role of supporting the armed forces and security of allies, but also as a means of pursuing wider foreign and security policy goals. First, in contrast to their traditional use as a means of counterbalancing enemies, military cooperation and assistance are now being used to help build cooperative relationships with former or potential enemies. This process is referred to here as strategic engagement. In terms of great-power relations, it is most obvious in the West's efforts to develop military cooperation with Russia and China. Similar processes are also observable at a regional level, for example between post-apartheid South Africa and its neighbours and between post-communist Poland and its neighbours. Second, in contrast to the past maintenance of military cooperation with authoritarian regimes, the Western democracies are increasingly using military cooperation and assistance to promote democratic civilian control of armed forces as part of wider efforts to support liberal democracy and good governance. Third, military cooperation and assistance have increasingly been used to support partner states in developing the capacity to contribute to peacekeeping and peace-enforcement operations. In particular, NATO has supported Eastern European states in developing peacekeeping capabilities, and the US, the UK and France have supported African states likewise.

It is thus possible to distinguish between old defence diplomacy, with its realpolitik emphasis on countering enemies, and new defence diplomacy, with its emphasis on engagement with potential enemies, support for democracy, good governance and human rights, and enabling states to deal with their own security problems. Since the 1990s, the balance in Western military cooperation and assistance policies has shifted away from the old and towards the new. Nevertheless, the new defence diplomacy exists alongside the old, and there are tensions between the two. Continuing efforts to strengthen the military capabilities of allies such as Japan and the new NATO members create problems in strategic engagement with China and Russia, while strategic engagement with China and Russia potentially risks undermining the ability to defend against these states should that be necessary. Western governments therefore face difficult dilemmas in balancing military cooperation with longstanding allies and efforts at strategic engagement with potential enemies. Similarly, while Western governments have paid more attention to the promotion of democratic civil–military relations in some regions, they also continue in some cases to pursue military cooperation with authoritarian allies, most obviously Saudi Arabia and other Gulf states. At a minimum, this creates a double standard in Western policies; at worst, it risks undermining the more general basis of the new defence diplomacy. Moreover, since the September 2001 terrorist attacks there has been a shift away from the new defence diplomacy and back towards the old realpolitik defence diplomacy. As part of efforts to counter terrorism, the US and other states such as the UK and Australia have intensified military cooperation with, and provided significant new military assistance to, a number of countries, notably the Central Asian states, Indonesia and the Philippines, despite their (and especially their militaries') poor records on democracy and human rights.

The archetypal example of the new defence diplomacy is NATO's Partnership for Peace (PfP). PfP was established in 1994 to facilitate political and military cooperation between NATO and the countries of Central and Eastern Europe.[2] It is based on 'bilateral' agreements between NATO and each individual partner, allowing cooperation to be tailored to the needs and interests of the state concerned, although many activities are multilateral. PfP is widely viewed as a success story. It has helped to overcome the Cold War division of Europe; paved the way to full NATO membership for some states while maintaining cooperation with others; encouraged cooperation amongst Eastern European states; supported states in establishing democratic control of and reforming their militaries; facilitated the development of inter-operability with NATO; and contributed to the success of NATO's peacekeeping operations in the Balkans.

Most countries engage in a range of national defence diplomacy activities. In the decades after the Second World War, the US built up a range of global military cooperation and assistance relationships and programmes (see Table 2). During the 1990s, these activities were to various degrees redirected towards the new defence diplomacy goals identified above. The US played the leading role in the development of NATO's PfP, as well as in efforts to develop military cooperation with Russia and China.[3] A number of new programmes were established. In 1991, the Expanded International Military Education and Training (E-IMET) programme was set up to provide training for foreign military and civilian personnel in defence management, civil–military relations and military justice. An Enhanced International Peacekeeping Capabilities (EIPC) Initiative was established in 1996 to support states in developing the capacity to contribute to peacekeeping operations. The US has also sought to regionalise and multilateralise its defence diplomacy activities. Much US defence diplomacy is undertaken by its regional military commands: European Command (EUCOM, which has responsibility for Europe and, since 1999, Africa), Pacific Command (PACOM, with responsibility for the Asia–Pacific region), Central Command (CENTCOM, with responsibility for the Middle East) and Southern Command (SOUTHCOM, with responsibility for South America).

Table 2: **US military cooperation and assistance programmes**
• International Military Education and Training (IMET): the primary programme supporting the training of foreign military personnel (and a limited number of civilians) at US military training and education institutions; also provides US military training and education in other countries. Funding for the 2000 financial year was $49.8 million, and the programme has provided training for over 9,000 people.
• Expanded IMET (E-IMET): a sub-programme of IMET, mandated by the US Congress in 1991, which focuses on non-combat and non-technical training in areas such as defence management, civil–military relations and military justice; approximately 30% of IMET-funded courses fall into the E-IMET category.
• Foreign Military Interaction (FMI): a programme supporting a wide range of military-to-military contacts with other states.
• Foreign Military Financing (FMF): grants and loans to help other states to buy US military equipment, defence services and training; primarily supports arms transfers to other states, but also supports training and other activities. FMF funding in FY2000 was $4.79 billion.
• Joint Combined Exchange Training (JCET): a programme allowing US special forces to train with or provide training to foreign militaries overseas.
• Foreign Military Sales (FMS): the main programme for government-to-government sales of weapons to other states; the Department of Defense serves as an intermediary and often provides maintenance and training. Sales in FY2000 were approximately $12.1bn.
• 'Emergency drawdown' and Excess Defense Articles (EDA): programmes allowing the US government to transfer weapons and training to other states in emergency circumstances or to dispose of surplus military equipment; in FY2000 drawdowns worth $80.6m and EDA worth $433m were transferred.
• Enhanced International Peacekeeping Capabilities (EIPC) Initiative: an initiative designed to enhance the ability of other states to contribute to international peacekeeping missions; currently providing support to 20 countries, including Argentina, Bangladesh, Poland, South Africa and Ukraine. Supported by $2.5m of FMF funds in FY2000.

Sources: 'Foreign Military Assistance', Appendix M in Department of Defense, *US Annual Defense Review 2001* (Washington DC: Department of Defense, 2001); and Adam Isacson and Joy Olson, *Just the Facts: A Civilian's Guide to US Defense and Security Assistance to Latin America and the Caribbean* (Washington DC: Latin America Working Group in cooperation with the Center for International Policy, November 2001), www.ciponline.org/facts.

The US has also sponsored the establishment of a number of regional centres as frameworks for defence dialogue and training: the US–German Marshall Centre for European Security Studies, based in Germany, which provides training for military personnel from post-communist Europe; the Asia–Pacific Center for Security Studies, based in Honolulu; and the Center for Hemispheric Defense Studies, the African Center for Strategic Studies and the Near East South Asia Center for Strategic Studies, all based at the US National Defense University in Washington DC.

The UK has the most developed concept of defence diplomacy. The 1998 Strategic Defence Review made defence diplomacy one of eight core missions of British defence policy.[4] The British concept is divided into three elements: an outreach programme of cooperation with the countries of Central and Eastern Europe; defence diplomacy activities in other parts of the world; and arms control, non-proliferation and confidence-building.[5] The UK has played a leading role in developing defence diplomacy cooperation with the countries of post-communist Europe, as well as building on longer-standing defence ties with countries in the Middle East and Africa in particular. The UK has also sought to integrate the Ministry of Defence's defence diplomacy with the parallel activities of the Foreign and Commonwealth Office and the Department for International Development through the creation of a shared Global Conflict Prevention fund.

Other European governments have also developed new defence diplomacy initiatives since the 1990s. France, which had maintained close defence ties with its former colonies, has devoted greater attention to Central and Eastern Europe; within Africa, it has shifted from the more narrow promotion of French economic interests, such as arms sales, to wider goals, including the promotion of democratic civil–military relations and support for the development of regional peacekeeping capabilities. Germany has developed a wide range of bilateral defence cooperation activities with the countries of Central and Eastern Europe, especially its immediate neighbours Poland and the Czech Republic, as well as Russia, as a means of promoting reform and improving historically troubled relations with these states. Other West European countries have developed similar programmes, often on the basis of special relationships with their eastern neighbours: Norway with Russia in relation to their far northern border, Denmark with the Baltic states and Italy with the Balkan countries. The European neutral states have also developed specific initiatives: Finland and Sweden with the Baltic states; Austria with Hungary, Croatia and Slovenia; Switzerland through the specialised work of the Geneva Centre for Security Policy, the Geneva Centre for Democratic Control of the

Armed Forces and the Geneva International Centre for Humanitarian Demining. Although themselves recipients of PfP-type assistance, Central and Eastern European states have also developed defence diplomacy cooperation with their neighbours. Poland and Hungary, for example, have actively used military cooperation as a means of improving relations with their eastern and southern neighbours.

Elsewhere in the world, the expansion of defence diplomacy has not been as dramatic, but there have nevertheless been significant developments. In Asia, the US has sought to use defence diplomacy as one means of building new cooperative relationships with China and India. The ASEAN Regional Forum (ARF) has initiated cautious moves towards multilateral security dialogue in the Asia–Pacific, supplemented by a track-two process of cooperation amongst security studies institutes within the region. As part of its wider strategy of intensified engagement, Australia has developed new military ties with Indonesia and China, and has undertaken efforts to help the smaller Pacific Island states in areas such as peacekeeping and the security of arms stockpiles. With the revision of its defence guidelines, Japan is also slowly beginning to pursue bilateral and multilateral defence dialogue and exchanges with neighbouring states, including China and South Korea. In the Americas, OAS defence ministers have met a number of times since the mid-1990s, and have taken some limited steps towards further multilateral defence cooperation; new bilateral defence cooperation relationships have been established (notably between Argentina and Brazil); and longstanding US defence ties with its southern neighbours have been reoriented towards new objectives, including the promotion of democratic civil–military relations, as well as cooperation in the 'war on drugs' and the 'war on terror'. In Africa, the AU and subregional groups such as SADC have begun processes of multilateral defence cooperation, including meetings of officials and holding multilateral military exercises. The US, the UK and France are providing assistance to help African states develop indigenous peacekeeping activities.

This paper analyses the new defence diplomacy as it has emerged since the 1990s; explores the problems and dilemmas involved in the new uses to which military cooperation and assistance are being put; and assesses the role of defence diplomacy in the international security environment post-September 2001. In particular, it seeks to answer a number of questions. What potential limitations and dilemmas does the new defence diplomacy present as opposed to the old realpolitik purposes to which military cooperation and assistance were put in the past? Is the new defence diplomacy likely to be a lasting development, or merely a transitional phenomenon of the post-Cold War era? To what extent is the new defence diplomacy a primarily European phenomenon, reflecting the particular circumstances of post-Cold War Europe, with limited relevance for other regions? To what extent is the US-led 'war on terror' likely to lead to a shift back to older realpolitik patterns of defence diplomacy, and what role is defence diplomacy likely to play in the new security environment of the early twenty-first century?

Chapter one examines the role of defence diplomacy as a means of strategic engagement between former or potential enemies, and explores the lessons to be learned from Western efforts to develop military cooperation with Russia and China since the mid-1990s. Chapter two examines the role of defence diplomacy in promoting democratic civil–military relations, exploring the lessons from a decade of PfP engagement on this issue in Central and Eastern Europe, and the more problematic role of the US in relation to democracy and civil–military relations in South America. Chapter three examines the role of defence diplomacy in supporting other states in developing peacekeeping and enforcement capabilities, exploring the lessons from PfP support in this area in Central and Eastern Europe, and Western efforts to support the development of African peacekeeping capabilities over the last decade. The conclusion returns to the wider question of the scope and significance of defence diplomacy in the contemporary security environment.

This paper argues that the changes in patterns of international defence diplomacy since the 1990s are a genuinely new and significant development, with lasting relevance. In effect, the new defence diplomacy suggests that, alongside their traditional role as an instrument for the use of force, armed forces and defence ministries also have an important role to play as a tool for cooperative peacetime engagement with other states. The three new roles of defence diplomacy identified in this paper – strategic engagement as a means of reducing the likelihood of conflict between former or potential enemies; promoting democratic civil–military relations; and supporting other states in developing peacekeeping capabilities – are likely to have continued relevance in various parts of the world.

The new defence diplomacy, however, will continue to run alongside the old realpolitik version, and tensions between the two will remain. For the US, where the shift away from the new defence diplomacy has been especially pronounced, military cooperation with allies in the 'war on terror' is likely to remain a priority, and the other goals of the new defence diplomacy will be relatively less important. Nevertheless, the goals and means of the new defence diplomacy remain, even if they have a somewhat lower priority. Moreover, the 'war on terror' has also led to a recognition that weak states and regions of conflict can be a source of terrorism. Defence diplomacy is thus likely to have a continuing role as one of the tools for helping to stabilise weak states, promote democracy and reduce the likelihood of conflict in regions of tension.

Chapter 1

Strategic Engagement: Defence Diplomacy as a Means of Conflict Prevention

One of the major changes in patterns of defence diplomacy since the early 1990s has been the increasing use of military cooperation and assistance. Their rise, however, has not come about through their traditional role as a means of strengthening allies' defence capabilities, but rather as an instrument for attempting to build cooperative relations with former or potential adversaries, and thereby helping to prevent potential conflicts. This paper refers to this process as strategic engagement. At the major power level, the US and its allies have used defence diplomacy as a component of wider policies designed to improve relations with Russia and China. Australia has used it as a means of engaging Indonesia; it was employed as a means of overcoming the historic conflict between Argentina and Brazil; and Balkan states such as Bulgaria and Romania have used it as part of efforts to avoid conflict. This chapter examines the use of defence diplomacy as a means of improving relations and preventing conflict with potential enemies, explores the lessons that may be learned from the West's military engagement with Russia and China since the 1990s and concludes by assessing the wider relevance of defence diplomacy as a tool of conflict prevention.

As an instrument for building cooperation and preventing conflict between former or potential adversaries, defence diplomacy works in a number of different ways and operates on a number of different levels:

- Military cooperation can perform a primarily political role, acting as a symbol of willingness to pursue broader cooperation, mutual trust and commitment to work to overcome or manage differences.

- Military cooperation can be a means of introducing transparency into defence relations, in particular with regard to states' intentions and capabilities. High-level discussions of defence policy and military doctrine can be used to show that a state does not have offensive intentions and that its armed forces are primarily defensive in character, thereby offering reassurance to, and building confidence with, the partner state.

- Defence diplomacy can be a means of building or reinforcing perceptions of common interests. Western efforts to engage Russia in practical cooperation in peacekeeping and counter-terrorism, for example, have been not simply about strengthening or reforming Russian capabilities in these areas, but also about reinforcing the perception that Russia and the West share common interests which should be addressed through international partnership.

- Military cooperation is also about changing the mind-sets of partner states' militaries. Much of Western defence diplomacy towards Russia and China implicitly aims to alter the perception within these countries' armed forces of the US/the West as a threat, for example by explaining Western intentions and capabilities, emphasising common interests and high-lighting the shared challenges facing military professionals. Lord Robertson, architect of the British concept of defence diplomacy as Secretary of State for Defence during the UK's 1998 Strategic Defence Review and subsequently NATO Secretary-General, has described this process as 'disarmament of the mind'.[1]

- Military cooperation may be used to support specific, concrete defence reforms in the partner state. The West, for example, has put considerable resources into supporting the rehousing of Russian troops withdrawn from the former Soviet empire and retraining demobilised soldiers. Again, such cooperation not only contributes to the direct objective concerned, but also helps to change perceptions and build support within the Russian military for cooperation with the West.

- Defence assistance may also be used as an incentive to

encourage partner states to cooperate in other areas. At a strategic level, defence-related assistance may be made conditional on or linked to partner states' behaviour on other issues. In the early 1990s, US defence assistance to Ukraine was linked to Kiev's denuclearisation. At a micro level, exchanges of military officers and attendance at training courses and conferences in the West are sometimes derided as 'military tourism', but often provide individual service personnel and civilian defence officials with a direct and personal stake in cooperation with the West.

The use of military cooperation as a tool for building confidence and improving broader political relations with potential adversaries raises a number of problems and dilemmas. Behind the use of military cooperation as a means of strategic engagement lie major questions about the causes of international conflict and the connection between military power and political relations between states. To the extent that conflicts between states result from mutual uncertainties about each other's intentions, the threatening potential of other states' military power or historically inherited mistrust, then military cooperation may be effective. To the extent that conflicts between states result from real and substantive *political* differences, whether over specific issues such as territory and borders or over wider questions such as the norms underpinning international politics or the international balance of power, the utility of military cooperation as a means of promoting mutual confidence and improving political relations is likely to be limited.

The West's relations with Russia and China reflect these underlying problems: while in both cases military cooperation has the potential to generate mutual reassurance and help to overcome historic mistrust, there are also substantive political differences (for example, over the future of the former Soviet republics or Taiwan) which cannot easily be overcome by defence diplomacy. Elsewhere, Indo–Pakistani tensions reflect not just historic mistrust and the mutual threat posed by each other's military, but also the unresolved status of Kashmir. Similarly, although military cooperation might be able to help reduce tensions between China and its South-east Asian neighbours, it is unlikely to overcome their disputes over the Spratly and Paracel islands.

The nature of defence policy and the military profession poses an additional obstacle to the successful use of defence diplomacy as a means of building sustainable cooperation with putative adversaries. The fundamental goal of defence policy is to defend the country against attack, and this involves at least considering, and often preparing for, worst-case scenarios. Similarly, the central purpose of the military profession is to prepare for and engage in war-fighting. While military contacts and transparency can help to reduce misperceptions and mistrust, they are unlikely to fully overcome the tendency of defence planners and service personnel to prepare for the worst. Nor will contacts between professional soldiers necessarily prevent armed conflict if this is the direction in which political and military leaders wish to go.

A second set of dilemmas revolves around the issue of conditionality: to what extent, and how, should military cooperation be linked to a partner's cooperation on other issues, its domestic behaviour or its undertaking of specific reforms? Strategic engagement can be viewed as a long-term, gradual process of promoting change in partners' perceptions and policies by engaging them. From this perspective, sustained engagement may be the key to success, suggesting that cooperation should not be linked too closely to short-term developments, made overly conditional on specific reforms or broken off in the face of temporary setbacks.

The use of defence diplomacy as a tool for strategic engagement involves a number of conditionality dilemmas. First, to the extent that defence diplomacy involves making defence policy and activities more transparent, how far should this be dependent on reciprocity? If the primary aim is to reassure or build confidence with a potential enemy, it may be argued that opening up one's defence policy and military can help to achieve this goal, regardless of whether the other state does likewise. If defence diplomacy is viewed as a mutual process, however, then reciprocity is important. Furthermore, unilateral 'concessions' may be difficult to sustain domestically, and the transparency implicit in defence diplomacy may be vulnerable to exploitation. Chinese civilian and military officials engaged in defence cooperation activities with the US have, for example, been accused of spying against America. Defence diplomacy as a means of strategic engagement with potential enemies inevitably involves striking a balance between offering reassurance and transparency on the one hand, and building a reciprocal process on the other.

Second, how far should defence diplomacy cooperation be conditional on partners' domestic behaviour with regard to human rights and democracy? To the extent that the primary goal is to prevent conflict, then defence diplomacy arguably should not be made dependent on a partner state improving its record on human rights or democracy. In the long term, moreover, the process of strategic engagement may do more for human rights and democracy than short-term sanctions or the suspension of defence diplomacy cooperation. Maintaining cooperation with authoritarian states, however, risks giving them at least implicit political and military support. In the early and mid-1990s, for example, Australia invested significant efforts in defence diplomacy as a means of improving relations with Indonesia, yet this did little to improve the human-rights situation in the country, nor did it prevent the vicious Indonesian behaviour in East Timor in 1999.[2] Again, there is a difficult balance to strike between the strategic aim of preventing conflict with a potential enemy, and concern for human rights and democracy (this issue is revisited in chapter two).

Third, how far should defence diplomacy cooperation be linked to partner states' behaviour on wider issues, such as regional conflicts or efforts to prevent the proliferation of weapons of mass destruction, beyond the direct bilateral relationship concerned? The answer to this question is likely to depend on the relative importance of the different goals involved, but will again entail difficult decisions. Given that all these various conditionality dilemmas involve balancing competing objectives in diverse circumstances, they are likely to be a persistent feature of debates on the use of defence diplomacy, and cannot be definitively resolved.

Western military cooperation with Russia

Since the early 1990s, the West has used defence diplomacy as part of its wider efforts to build a cooperative relationship with post-communist Russia. The implicit aim of Western defence diplomacy has been to help prevent conflict with Russia and make the country a long-term partner of the West. Military cooperation between the Soviet Union and the West can be traced back to the Confidence and Security Building Measures (CSBMs) of the 1970s; it expanded during the Gorbachev era in the 1980s, and intensified significantly after the collapse of the Soviet Union in 1991.[3]

Western military cooperation with post-Soviet Russia has developed along two inter-related tracks: multilateral engagement with NATO, and bilateral links with individual Western states. NATO–Russia military cooperation evolved gradually during the 1990s, reflecting continuing Russian ambivalence about NATO. Initial contacts were established in 1993–94, Russia joined NATO's PfP in 1994–95 and the NATO–Russia Founding Act on Mutual Relations, Cooperation and Security was signed in May 1997.[4] The Founding Act included a significant defence cooperation dimension, but its implementation proved problematic. In 1995, Russia agreed to contribute forces to NATO's Implementation/Stabilisation Force (I/SFOR) peacekeeping operation in Bosnia, and this was followed by a similar agreement to contribute to the Kosovo Force (KFOR) operation in 1999. NATO's 1999 intervention in Kosovo, however, led Russia to suspend almost all cooperation with the Alliance, although this was gradually re-established afterwards. The September 2001 terrorist attacks and Russian President Vladimir Putin's subsequent reorientation of Russia towards the West resulted in a significant improvement in NATO–Russia relations, with the establishment of the new NATO–Russia Council – which brings together NATO and Russia on a regular basis – in 2002. Defence cooperation has also intensified. The US, the UK, Germany and other NATO members have also concluded various bilateral defence cooperation agreements with Russia, and much actual cooperation takes place bilaterally.

In terms of substance, Western defence diplomacy towards Russia over the last decade has involved a wide range of activities:

- Regular meetings of senior civilian defence officials and military personnel, with discussion of both general issues and specific cooperative activities.
- Discussions of defence policy, force structure and related issues.
- Lower-level military-to-military contacts, including exchanges of officers and units and port visits.
- Participation of Russian officers in training courses in the West.
- Russian participation in bilateral and multilateral military exercises, primarily relating to humanitarian missions, disaster relief, search and rescue at sea, peacekeeping and other non-combat tasks.

- Russian participation in the SFOR and KFOR operations, which involved wide-ranging operational cooperation and the negotiation of special command arrangements.
- Western support for the resettlement of soldiers withdrawn from Central and Eastern Europe and the former Soviet republics, and the retraining of demobilised soldiers.
- Western support for Russian efforts to reduce and secure control of its arsenal of nuclear, biological and chemical weapons and related infrastructure, primarily through the US Nunn–Lugar Cooperative Threat Reduction (CTR) programme.

After a decade of military cooperation with post-communist Russia, a number of conclusions may be drawn. Russian political and military leaders have, to varying degrees, been wary of and resistant to defence cooperation with the West. Russia prevaricated over whether to join the PfP in 1994–95, and cut off most cooperation in response to NATO's intervention in Kosovo. During the 1990s, NATO officials often expressed disappointment at Russia's reluctance to use the opportunities created by the PfP and the NATO–Russia Founding Act to enable more substantive discussion of defence issues.[5] Observers argue that the senior Russian military leaders who control the country's Ministry of Defence have generally been reluctant to support defence cooperation with the West, and prevent their subordinates from engaging in such activities.[6]

Defence cooperation has also not been able to avert or overcome serious political differences over issues such as NATO enlargement and the Alliance's Balkan interventions. For much of the 1990s, Russia's relations with the West veered between cooperation and a threatened 'Cold Peace'. At the lowest point, during the 'race for Pristina' at the end of the Kosovo war in June 1999 – when 200 Russian paratroopers were rushed to the capital of Kosovo ahead of NATO forces – it appeared that Russian and NATO forces might clash directly. Despite these problems, however, Western defence cooperation with Russia was never completely derailed. When Russia broke off relations with NATO in 1999, for example, some elements of bilateral military cooperation were maintained with individual NATO members, as was cooperation in SFOR.

The elements of defence cooperation that are generally perceived to have been most successful involve the most substantive practical activities, in particular Russia's involvement in the SFOR and KFOR missions, Western support for the resettlement and retraining of Russian soldiers and efforts to secure control of former Soviet WMD. Russia's SFOR and KFOR involvement included both high-level political–military cooperation, in terms of negotiating and operating the command and control arrangements for the integration of Russian forces, and lower-level operational cooperation on the ground. Through their programmes to support resettlement and retraining, Germany, the UK and the US have helped Moscow to peacefully implement its strategic military withdrawal from Central Europe and the Baltic states, and greatly reduce the size of the Russian military. Through the CTR programme and related efforts, the West has also helped Moscow to transfer all tactical nuclear weapons back to Russia, reduce the Russian nuclear arsenal and strengthen controls over remaining weapons. During the 2001 US-led intervention in Afghanistan, Russia worked closely with the US in intelligence, supplying the US-backed Northern Alliance with weapons and coordinating Northern Alliance operations on the ground. The key lesson of these successes is that initiatives designed to address substantive problems and real common interests provide a more durable basis for cooperation than primarily symbolic activities undertaken for the sake of cooperation. Such initiatives create strong incentives for reluctant partners to engage, and not only address the specific problem at hand, but also contribute to wider confidence-building.

Despite a decade of engagement, however, the impact of Western defence diplomacy on Russian defence policy and the Russian military has been limited. While Russian defence policy has undergone radical change since the early 1990s, that change has been driven primarily by the consequences of the Soviet Union's breaking up, Russia's dire economic circumstances and the consequent rapid and broadly based deprofessionalisation of its armed forces.[7] A decade of Western military outreach has not yet persuaded many Russian decision-makers, especially in the military, that the US and NATO are not a threat. Russia's national security strategy and military doctrine adopted in 2000 are based on the assumption of conflict between a US-led West and countries such as Russia supporting a multipolar world.[8] Similarly, Russian civil–military relations remain far from Western standards of democratic civilian control.[9] The Russian armed forces are enmeshed in domestic politics through the elected presence of many serving officers in the *Duma* (parliament), and the senior military's position as one of the forces which supported Putin's rise to power. The Ministry of Defence remains an essentially military institution, with at best limited civilian control of policy, and the senior Russian military remains one of the more conservative, anti-Western forces within the Russian policy-making elite. As one Russian observer has put it, the Russian military leadership 'is determined to build national security *against* NATO as much as *with* it'.[10]

The September 2001 terrorist attacks on the US resulted in a significant improvement in relations between Russia and the West, especially the US. Putin appears to have taken a strategic decision to reorient Russia towards the West, resulting in Russian support for the US in Afghanistan, a restrained response to the US decision in 2001 to withdraw from the Anti-Ballistic Missile (ABM) Treaty, acquiescence to NATO's 2002 invitation to seven Eastern European countries (including the three Baltic states) to join the Alliance and the establishment of the NATO–Russia Council. Russia's opposition to the Iraq war in 2003, however, showed the limits of this rapprochement, and suggested that Russia might strengthen ties with those European states (especially Germany and France) pursuing greater independence from the US. Given that many in Russia, especially within the military, continue to view the US, the West and NATO as antagonists more than partners, observers have argued that Putin's reorientation of foreign policy rests on a weak domestic base.

Nonetheless, the post-September 2001 improvement in relations has created a more solid basis for defence cooperation. The NATO–Russia Council has provided a new political impetus and institutional framework, and counter-terrorism has provided a new focus – one based on strong perceptions of a common security interest. The US and other Western states are now engaging with the Russian military on counter-terrorism in a way that was not the case before September 2001. The US–Russian strategic nuclear relationship is also shifting away from old-style arms control towards less formal defence diplomacy-type cooperation. The 2001–02 Strategic Offensive Reduction Treaty (SORT) negotiations resulted in a much looser treaty framework than previous talks, but also the establishment of working groups to discuss various defence cooperation issues.[11] Discussions in these working groups have focused on 'transparency and predictability' in regard to strategic nuclear force reductions through measures such as detailed exchanges of information, visits to nuclear weapon sites and cooperative activities at such sites. According to US Under-Secretary of Defense for Policy Douglas Feith, the US is aiming to 'develop a more cooperative relationship, where we on a regular basis are exchanging information on these things in the way that we exchange information with other friends and allies'.[12]

The longer-term future of Russia's relations with the West, nevertheless, remains uncertain. Each side arguably has strong common interests in managing European security and countering terrorism and proliferation, and Russia needs Western trade and investment. Nevertheless, many Russians remain wary of what they see as Western encroachment in their traditional sphere of influence, and are inclined to build countervailing alliances against the West, especially the US. Russian policies in some areas, such as exports of nuclear technology to Iran, are also likely to generate tensions. Defence diplomacy is thus likely to remain an important – if sometimes problematic – part of Western efforts to build a lasting partnership with Russia.

US military cooperation with China

Over the last decade, there has been much debate over how other states should respond to the rising economic, political and military power of China. US policy has been pulled between attempts to contain China and efforts to engage it and thereby build a cooperative relationship with Beijing. Military cooperation has been one of the means used by the US in its attempts to engage.[13] US military cooperation with communist China can be traced back to 1980. Following America's formal diplomatic recognition of the People's Republic in 1979, the US initiated military cooperation as part of its broader normalisation of relations with Beijing.[14] In response to the 1989 Tiananmen Square massacre, however, the US suspended all high-level official exchanges, including military contacts, and banned the sale of arms to China. Political and military contacts were only gradually re-established in the early 1990s.[15]

The Clinton administration's China policy reflected the tensions in US attitudes towards Beijing. Despite concerns over China's growing economic and military power, the administration gradually developed a policy of 'comprehensive engagement', culminating in summits between Clinton and Chinese President Jiang Zemin in the US in October 1997, and in China in June 1998. Defence diplomacy developed slowly, and was bedevilled by a number of disputes and disruptions. US Secretary of Defense William Perry did not visit China until October 1994. A return visit by Perry's Chinese counterpart, General Chi Haotian, was delayed until late 1996 by disputes over Taiwan (including the March 1996 crisis, when the US sent two carrier battle groups to the region in response to Chinese missile tests and ground force exercises close to Taiwan).[16] Although more substantive cooperation subsequently developed, China suspended military exchanges with the US following the bombing of the Chinese Embassy in Belgrade in May 1999, during NATO's intervention in Kosovo. Military ties were re-established in 2000.[17] Military cooperation has also been constrained by US concerns over China's human-rights record, Beijing's role as a proliferator of ballistic missiles and weapons of mass destruction and Chinese espionage in the US. The Bush administration initially spoke of China as a 'strategic competitor', and on coming to power in 2001 Defense Secretary Donald Rumsfeld froze military exchanges pending a policy review.[18] Relations were further undermined by an incident in April 2001 when a US EP-3 surveillance aircraft collided with a Chinese F-8 fighter in airspace off the Chinese coast and China detained the American aircraft and its crew.[19] The September 2001 terrorist attacks on the US, however, led to an improvement in relations, with China offering some political and practical support.[20] Sino-US military cooperation since the 1990s has included:[21]

- High-level political discussions, including reciprocal visits by defence ministers, their deputies and other senior officials, annual Defense Consultation Talks, initiated in December 1997, and transparency briefings between the Chinese military and the US Department of Defense.
- High-level military exchanges, including visits by high-ranking US military personnel to previously unseen Chinese military installations.
- Professional exchanges between military educational institutions, such as the two countries' defence universities.
- A 1998 Military Maritime Consultation Agreement to prevent incidents at sea, with subsequent working group meetings on the implementation of the agreement.

- Reciprocal port visits by warships.
- Discussion of mutual approaches to humanitarian assistance and disaster relief.
- Agreement on mutual observation of military exercises.
- An agreement (reached during Clinton's 1998 visit to China) to 'de-target' strategic nuclear missiles.

Compared with Russia, US military cooperation with China has been more limited in scale and less substantive in nature. There have been significantly fewer meetings of senior defence officials and exchanges of military personnel. Secretary of Defense Perry noted that, in four years, he had been able to arrange only two meetings with his Chinese counterpart, and 'these were not really enough to develop a strong working relationship such as I had established in a dozen meetings with Russian Defense Minister Pavel Grachev'.[22] Similarly, while several thousand Russian soldiers now have experience of meeting and working with their Western counterparts, relatively few Chinese service personnel have had similar experiences. There are no equivalents in Sino–US military cooperation of the sort of detailed operational or functional cooperation between Russia and the West in SFOR and KFOR, the retraining and resettlement of Russian troops or the CTR programme.

The limited nature of Sino–US military cooperation reflects a number of factors. Relations between China and the US have become more, not less, problematic since the end of the Cold War, with disputes over a wide range of issues. The political and strategic context for military cooperation has therefore been less propitious than in the Russian case. Substantive political differences – in particular over the US military presence in Asia, Taiwan and China's role as a weapons proliferator – have constrained the development of military cooperation. The Chinese military, an insular institution heavily shaped by its communist heritage, has also been a 'passive and often reluctant partner', with the US frequently frustrated with the lack of reciprocity and transparency from Chinese counterparts.[23]

A number of conclusions may be drawn from the experience of the 1990s. First, as with Russia, military cooperation has not averted or overcome serious political differences. Second, Beijing and Washington continue to view each other as threats, and this inevitably constrains military cooperation. Third, the Chinese military remains reluctant to provide detailed information about defence policy or access to military installations, or to engage in bilateral or multilateral activities that involve a greater degree of openness.

Despite these problems, US efforts at engaging China militarily over the last decade can claim some success. First, although progress is limited and slow, the Chinese military is gradually opening itself up. The publication of the first Chinese defence white paper in 1998 was a significant step in this direction. The various defence cooperation activities with the US have involved an important increase in transparency compared with past practice. Second, during the 1990s China joined the majority of international non-proliferation regimes, including the Nuclear Non-Proliferation Treaty, the Missile Technology Control Regime, the Chemical Weapons Convention, the Comprehensive Test Ban Treaty and the Zangger Committee, which controls the export of nuclear weapons-related technologies. Although serious concerns remain about China's proliferation practices, accession to these core regimes was nonetheless a significant step. Third, given concerns about a possible Cold War-style confrontation, relations between the US and China could have become much worse since the 1990s, and America's defence diplomacy engagement has arguably helped to forestall this. In this context, defence diplomacy is likely to remain one element of continuing US efforts to encourage China towards partnership, rather than competition.

Conclusion

This chapter has examined the use of defence diplomacy as a means of building confidence and cooperation between former or potential adversaries, thereby helping to prevent conflict – a process this Paper refers to as strategic engagement. Defence diplomacy can contribute to conflict prevention in a number of ways: signalling a political commitment to develop cooperative relations, promoting military transparency and reducing misperceptions, promoting perceptions of common interests and socialising militaries towards cooperation.

Over the last decade, the most prominent examples of defence diplomacy as a means of strategic engagement have been Western efforts to develop military cooperation with Russia and China. Given the ambiguous nature of the West's relations with both countries, defence diplomacy is likely to remain an important part of wider Western efforts to build cooperative relations and prevent conflict.

The use of defence diplomacy as a means of conflict prevention is not, however, limited to great power relations. A number of other countries now actively use defence diplomacy in this way, and this should be supported. In Asia, for example, Japan should be encouraged to develop defence diplomacy engagement with its historic enemies China and South Korea. In Europe, countries such as Poland and Romania should be helped, as they integrate with NATO, in maintaining and expanding defence diplomacy with their eastern neighbours. In situations of intense hostility or conflict, such as between Israel and its Arab neighbours, defence diplomacy engagement is likely to be either impossible to establish or ineffective if attempted. Conversely, where states have stable, peaceful relations, the use of defence diplomacy as a means of conflict prevention is likely to be unnecessary (although states may have other reasons, such as common external interests, for pursuing defence cooperation). Many regional and bilateral relationships, however, lie between these extremes of enmity and amity. In these circumstances, defence diplomacy is a potentially useful tool of conflict prevention, and it should be creatively pursued. External powers may have an important role to play in this process by pressing states to pursue such strategic engagement, and by acting as neutral facilitators.

The Russian and Chinese cases suggest that the success of defence diplomacy as a tool of conflict prevention is dependent on wider political relations between the states concerned. Where there are substantive political differences, defence diplomacy is unlikely to overcome them. Successful defence diplomacy may also be partly dependent on the compatibility of the domestic political values of the states concerned, which helps to explain why it has progressed further between Russia and the West than between the US and China. Nevertheless, even where there are real political differences, defence diplomacy can help to reduce misunderstanding and mistrust. In the long run, it may also help to pave the way for the resolution of such differences.

The Russian and Chinese cases also show that defence diplomacy should be viewed as a long-term – decades-long – process, rather than an approach likely to produce quick results. Threat perceptions shaped by decades, and sometimes centuries, of conflict are difficult to alter and will change only slowly. Encouraging states to build armed forces that are transparent and non-threatening towards their neighbours is likely to be a similarly long-term process. Given such timescales, the use of defence diplomacy as a means of conflict prevention will inevitably be a difficult process, with periodic setbacks. Generational change may, however, be a key factor: when political and military leaders who emerged during periods of conflict or confrontation are replaced by younger counterparts, the prospects for new relationships may improve.

A number of conclusions may also be drawn about how best to utilise defence diplomacy as a tool of conflict prevention. Common interests should be emphasised as a basis. Functional cooperation and substantive projects may provide a more durable foundation and have a greater impact than more symbolic measures. Multilateral frameworks, such as regional organisations, should be used to encourage and legitimise defence diplomacy. Leaders need to build domestic support for it in order to ensure that it is not unnecessarily derailed. In the final analysis, however, defence diplomacy should be viewed as only one part of wider strategies for preventing conflict between former or potential enemies.

Chapter 2

Promoting Democratic Civil–Military Relations

The second key purpose to which Western governments have put defence diplomacy since the 1990s is the promotion of democratic civil–military relations. This is not entirely new. The US (and to some extent other countries) played an important role in the democratic rebuilding of the German and Japanese militaries after the Second World War, as well as in a number of later cases, such as Spain in the 1980s. Nevertheless, the promotion of democracy has become much more central to Western foreign policies since the 1990s, and defence diplomacy has increasingly been used as a means of promoting democratic civil–military relations.[1] This shift reflects a number of factors. First, the so-called 'third wave' of democratisation has seen transitions from authoritarianism to democracy in Southern Europe, South America, East Asia, Central and Eastern Europe, the former Soviet Union and Africa since the 1970s, dramatically increasing the number of democratic or democratising states in the world.[2] These states have often faced significant challenges in establishing democratic civilian control of their militaries. Second, since the 1980s democracy has been an important element of many post-conflict peace processes. Within this context, the reintegration and democratisation of armed forces has become a significant component of international peace-building strategies. Third, the end of the Cold War altered the strategic environment shaping Western governments' policies, making them less willing to support authoritarian allies and pushing support for democracy up the policy agenda. As a consequence of the spread of democracy, there was also growing support for the hypothesis that democracies do not go to war with one another.[3] The promotion of democracy became seen not only as a means of supporting democratic values, but also of contributing to international security.[4] Against this background, in Eastern Europe, Africa and elsewhere, Western governments have sought to assist in depoliticising armed forces, civilianising defence ministries and securing more effective civilian control over defence expenditure and procurement.

The commitment by Western governments to use defence diplomacy as an instrument to promote democratic civil–military relations, however, faces a number of serious problems and dilemmas. Most importantly, Western support for democracy remains inconsistent and constrained by other competing interests – and defence diplomacy inevitably reflects this. Despite the end of the Cold War, Western governments continue to provide support, including military cooperation and assistance, to authoritarian regimes in various parts of the world. Most prominently, the need for secure access to oil supplies, stability in the Persian Gulf and the deterrence of Iraq and Iran have led the US, the UK and to some extent France to maintain close defence relations with Saudi Arabia and the other Gulf states (it remains to be seen whether the overthrow of Saddam Hussein in Iraq will produce a long-term change in this pattern). Similarly, Western governments have maintained ties with oil-rich Nigeria despite its military's poor record on democracy and human rights. The US has close military ties with Egypt and Jordan because of their roles as promoters of peace with Israel and their perceived positions as bastions against Islamic fundamentalism. In South America, the 'war on drugs' has resulted in close military cooperation between the US and some of its southern neighbours, but also a relative downgrading of the priority attached to democratising civil–military relations. Since September 2001, the US and other Western countries such as Australia, Britain and France have significantly strengthened military ties with Pakistan, Central Asian states, the Philippines, Algeria and other allies in the 'war on terrorism', despite their often poor records on democracy, human rights and civil–military relations.

The double-standard implicit in Western defence diplomacy – support for the democratisation of civil–military relations in some cases, close military cooperation with authoritarian regimes in others – has a number of negative effects. First, military cooperation with authoritarian regimes makes Western governments appear hypocritical. Second, it risks generating anti-Western feeling and creating the circumstances for regime collapse (as in Iran in 1979, and potentially in Saudi Arabia, Pakistan or Central Asia). Third, the competing objectives of Western defence diplomacy sometimes undermine each other in direct ways: cooperation with the military in relation to terrorism or counter-narcotics may reinforce their influence and thereby undermine prospects for the democratisation of civil–military relations. Western officials sometimes argue that engagement with the armed forces of authoritarian regimes can help to promote long-term democratic reform, or at least curb the excessive abuse of power by the military. Decades of Western military cooperation with countries like Turkey, Pakistan and the Gulf states has, however, failed to produce significant changes in civil–military relations. Indeed, by making military cooperation a central element of relations, the West may actually have reinforced the political power of these countries' armed forces.

The use of defence diplomacy to promote democratic civil–military relations is thus highly context-dependent. In entrenched authoritarian regimes, the prospects for the democratisation of civil–military relations are likely to be very limited. By contrast, in reforming regimes or countries undergoing democratic transitions, external defence diplomacy may play an important role in promoting democratic civil–military relations. Defence diplomacy may include political and material support for reformers and democrats, pressure to prevent a slide back into authoritarianism, the provision of models and examples of best practice, and practical technical and material assistance for the development of democratic institutions and norms. It might also include constructive engagement with groups – such as the military – that may oppose or be wary of democratic reform.

Defence diplomacy can help to promote the democratisation of civil–military relations in a number of specific areas:

- **Civilian political control over the military**: key challenges in this area include depoliticising the military; altering the constitution to entrench the principle of democratic civilian control; establishing a chain of command that unambiguously reflects this principle; and reforming or establishing controlling institutions (a national security council, a ministry of defence and the like).

- **Democratic civilian control over defence policy**: key challenges in this area include reforming and civilianising the institutions for the management of defence policy (in particular the ministry of defence); developing systems for the management and control of the defence budget and procurement; and training a new cadre of civilian officials.

- **Legislative/parliamentary oversight**: key challenges in this area include defining the powers of the legislature/parliament in relation to the armed forces and defence policy; establishing parliamentary foreign affairs, security and/or defence committees; ensuring the role of parliament in approving relevant legislation, appointments, the defence budget, and the overseas and domestic use of the military; enabling the legislature/parliament or its committees to have access to information, hold hearings and to interview personnel; and the publication of parliamentary reports.

- **Rule of law, human rights and justice**: key challenges in this area include ensuring the submission of the armed forces and the executive to the rule of law; reforming the relevant legal and judicial systems; developing a culture of respect for human rights within the armed forces; and the problematic issue of justice in relation to past crimes or abuses committed by the military.

- **Civil society engagement**: key challenges in this area include transparency and freedom of information in relation to the armed forces and the defence budget; the development of independent research institutes, think-tanks and advocacy and campaigning groups; and a free and independent media with expertise in defence and security.

External defence diplomacy can provide political support for reformers, offer models of good practice, tender advice and material support in relation to technical aspects of reforms, provide training for military and civilian personnel, and promote a broader socialisation in democratic norms. This chapter examines such Western efforts to support the democratisation of civil–military relations in two contrasting regions: post-communist Europe, where it has been a central element of Western defence diplomacy; and South America, where the issue has been only one part of wider US defence engagement.

NATO, Partnership for Peace and Democracy

During the 1990s the promotion of democratic civil–military relations in post-communist Europe became a central goal of NATO, in particular through the Partnership for Peace (PfP) and the Alliance's enlargement into Central and Eastern Europe. Although NATO had always in theory been an alliance of democracies, the promotion of democracy was not central to its role during the Cold War and the strategic goal of countering the Soviet Union led it to accept the authoritarian Salazar regime in Portugal and the military regimes in Greece and Turkey in the 1960s and 1970s.[5] With the end of the Cold War, the promotion of democratic civil–military relations became a key aim of NATO's new eastern outreach policies, and democratic civilian control of the military became a prerequisite for membership.[6] When the PfP was established in January 1994, ensuring the democratic control of defence forces was defined as one of the programme's key objectives.[7] Since then, almost all the states of post-communist Europe have joined the PfP (as of spring 2004, Bosnia and Herzegovina and Serbia and Montenegro are the only major European countries outside the PfP).

NATO and its member states have provided a wide range of support to PfP partners to help them reform their civil–military relations, focusing on areas such as constitutional frameworks for democratic control of the military, operational chains of command for political control of the military, the organisation and civilianisation of defence ministries, defence planning and budgeting, the rule of law and parliamentary accountability. The main forms of cooperation include:

- Conferences and seminars on issues relating to the democratic control of the armed forces and defence policy.
- Advice on specific issues, often through visits by civilian and military officials from NATO and its member states or visits by partner states' officials to the West.
- Placement of advisers from NATO members in key positions in partner states' ministries of defence and military staffs.
- Participation of partner states' civilian and military personnel at NATO's political headquarters in Brussels and the Supreme Headquarters Allied Powers Europe (SHAPE) in Mons, giving those personnel direct experience of NATO's model of multinational civil–military cooperation. Most partners have

permanent delegations at NATO headquarters, participate in the Partnership Coordination Cell within SHAPE, which provides the framework for practical military cooperation, and second staff to NATO's own multinational political and military staffs.

- The PfP Planning and Review Process (PARP), where partners coordinate their national defence planning with NATO, giving them experience of how NATO and its members undertake their own defence planning.
- Since 1999, a Membership Action Plan (MAP) to assist countries aspiring to join NATO to prepare for membership of the Alliance, including help in establishing 'appropriate democratic and civilian control of their armed forces'.[8]
- Participation in multinational military exercises and in SFOR and KFOR peace-support operations (again giving partner states direct experience of NATO's model of civil–military cooperation).

After a decade of civil–military reform and defence diplomacy in post-communist Europe, a number of conclusions may be drawn.[9] Despite fears of praetorianism in Central and Eastern Europe, armed forces have largely not intervened in domestic politics or emerged as central obstacles or threats to democratisation. In a core group of countries now in the process of joining NATO and the EU – Bulgaria, the Czech Republic, Estonia, Hungary, Latvia, Lithuania, Poland, Romania, Slovakia and Slovenia – the norm of armed forces as the apolitical servant of democratically elected civilian authorities has become entrenched, the military is no longer associated with the former communist (or any other) political party and the risk of military intervention in domestic politics is minimal. A number of factors explain this development. First, although the communist system was not democratic, it did establish the principle of civilian control of the military. Second, to the extent that armed forces were politicised their loyalty to the communist system was often superficial. As Polish President Lech Walesa put it in the early 1990s, the Polish military was like a radish: red (communist) on the outside, but white (Polish and national) on the inside.[10] Third, the general desire of these countries to integrate with the West has been a powerful force supporting democratisation, including in the area of civil–military relations. Fourth, NATO's PfP-related outreach activities have helped to reinforce and operationalise democratic civilian control of the military.

Establishing effective democratic and civilian control over defence *policy* has, however, proved more challenging. The communist system left a legacy of military domination of policy and weak or non-existent structures for civilian control. Indeed, for the core group of countries noted above, establishing effective structures for the control, management and oversight of defence policy has proved their main challenge in civil–military relations since the early 1990s. This has involved establishing high-level policymaking structures (national security councils and the like), undertaking strategic defence reviews, reforming and civilianising ministries of defence, introducing clear and appropriate divisions of labour between ministries of defence and military staffs, establishing mechanisms for the control and management of defence budgets, strengthening the capacity of legislatures (in particular parliamentary defence or security committees) to provide oversight of the executive's management of defence, and encouraging the development of non-governmental expertise capable of contributing to debates on defence policy. In these areas, cooperation with NATO through PfP was key in providing governments with external political support to push through difficult reforms and overcome military resistance, as well as affording expertise and advice on the development of new policymaking structures. By the end of the 1990s, the states aspiring to membership of NATO and the EU had all taken important steps in establishing structures for democratic civilian control of defence policy.

Civil–military relations in the former Soviet and Yugoslav states have developed along different lines to Central Europe. The dominant pattern of politics that emerged in most of these countries was one of strong – often authoritarian – presidential rule, with few if any parliamentary, judicial or legal counterweights. In this context, civilian executive control of the military (and other security services) was one of the key tools of presidential rule, but the military also retained considerable autonomy and influence. In Russia, the support of the 'power ministries' and the military vote have been central to the Yeltsin and Putin administrations. In Yugoslavia/Serbia-Montenegro and Croatia, close ties with the military were key elements of the Milosevic and Tudjman regimes. In these states, the military also retained a much greater degree of control over defence policy than in Central Europe, and efforts to assert civilian political control over defence policy (for example by subordinating general staffs to defence ministries and civilianising defence ministries) have been much more constrained.

NATO in turn has played a more limited role in promoting civil–military reform in Russia, Ukraine and the other former Soviet republics: these countries have been more wary of engagement with NATO, their militaries have tended to resist 'imposed' Western reforms and NATO's leverage over them has been weaker than in Central Europe. The same was true in Croatia and Yugoslavia/Serbia until the collapse of the Tudjman and Milosevic regimes in 1999 and 2000. Since then, Croatia has joined the PfP and, with NATO's support, is undertaking the types of reform implemented by the Central European states in the 1990s.[11] Serbia–Montenegro is now seeking membership of the PfP, but this remains dependent on its cooperation with the International Criminal Tribunal for the Former Yugoslavia (ICTY). It has initiated civil–military reforms, but given the military's central role in both the Milosevic regime and in the Balkan wars of the 1990s these may be more difficult than elsewhere in post-communist Europe. Bosnia also remains a special case because of the division of the country into two 'entities' – the Muslim-Croat Federation and the Serb Republika Srpska – with separate militaries.

NATO's efforts to promote democratic civil–military relations – and democracy more broadly – highlight the difficult issue of democratic conditionality. In general, NATO has not made PfP membership dependent on democracy or respect for human rights. Membership was offered to all European states, including the authoritarian regimes in Belarus, the Caucasus and Central Asia. Until recently, however, PfP cooperation with these countries was constrained both by their own limited interest in relations with NATO, and by reluctance within the Alliance to engage too deeply with them. The main exceptions to this lack of conditionality have been Croatia and Serbia-Montenegro, where PfP membership has been made conditional on progress in democratisation and cooperation with the ICTY.

In contrast to PfP, NATO has made membership of the Alliance dependent on the consolidation of democracy, including democratic control of the military. When Visegrad Group states the Czech Republic, Hungary and Poland were invited to join NATO in 1997, Slovakia, the fourth Visegrad member, was left out because of the authoritarian tendencies of its Prime Minister, Vladimir Meciar. Slovakia's exclusion probably contributed to Meciar's election defeat the following year. NATO has also demanded specific civil–military reforms from its candidates. In 1994, attempts by Walesa to gain the support of the military in struggles with his domestic political opponents led NATO governments to warn that this threatened Poland's prospects for membership of the Alliance; as a result, Poland clarified and consolidated the chain of command for control of the military and defence policy. Since then, and especially since the institution of the MAP in 1999 and in the run-up to the 2002 decision to invite seven countries (Bulgaria, Estonia, Latvia, Lithuania, Romania, Slovakia and Slovenia) to join the Alliance, NATO has made explicit and detailed demands, in particular with regard to clarifying chains of command and establishing control over defence budgets. The prospect of NATO membership has been a powerful inducement to candidate countries to implement reforms, underpinning the successful use of defence diplomacy.

The US-led 'war on terrorism' and NATO's 2002 decision to extend membership are likely to significantly reshape the Alliance's role in promoting the democratisation of civil–military relations. The 'war on terrorism' has added an important new dimension to NATO and especially US defence diplomacy in post-communist Eurasia. The US has significantly intensified military cooperation with and assistance to the Central Asian states, in particular Uzbekistan and Kyrgyzstan, in return for their support (including the provision of military base facilities) for the US intervention in Afghanistan and against terrorism and Islamic radicalism more generally.[12] The US has sent military advisers to train the Georgian armed forces fighting Chechen and Islamic militants in the Pankisi Gorge region bordering Chechnya. NATO has intensified its own military cooperation with the Central Asian and Caucasian states. This cooperation takes place notwithstanding the authoritarian nature of the Central Asian and Caucasian regimes, their poor human-rights records and the role that their armed forces and security services play as important pillars of authoritarian rule. Some suggest that defence diplomacy can help to moderate the behaviour of such regimes and be a long-term force for democratisation. Critics argue that the US, and to a lesser extent NATO as a whole, risks bolstering these regimes and, by closing down other avenues for dissent, making Islamic radicalism the only means of opposition.[13]

At the same time, the 2002 decision to extend NATO membership means that the Alliance's most active PfP partners and the states which have made most progress in democratising civil–military relations will become full NATO members. Although NATO's leverage over these states may decline once they do, they have already passed the key threshold of consolidating democratic civilian control of the military and defence policy. While NATO and its longer-standing members may continue to provide low-key assistance to new members in reforming civil–military relations, the issue is likely to be much less important than it was in the 1990s. Aside from the European neutral and non-aligned states, who may eventually opt to join NATO, most of the remaining PfP partners will be countries with more troubled democratic records and less interest in integrating with the West than the countries now in the process of joining NATO and the EU. Enlargement therefore may reinforce the shift in NATO/PfP defence diplomacy towards counter-terrorism and expanded ties with the Central Asian and Caucasian states. It remains to be seen how far such activities will become the core focus of NATO's PfP outreach, and to what extent the 'war on terrorism' will provide new reasons to overlook or subordinate the promotion of democracy. At a minimum, while the PfP may continue to act as a framework for promoting democratic civil–military relations, it will do so in more challenging and less amenable circumstances than in Central and Eastern Europe during the 1990s.

The US and South America

South America provides a key example of a region that has undergone democratisation since the 1970s, where governments have faced significant challenges in establishing democratic civilian control of the military and where a major external power – the US – has extensive defence diplomacy engagement. In contrast to post-communist Europe, however, the geostrategic and political context has been less propitious for the promotion of democratic civil–military relations, that goal has been less central to US defence diplomacy and other objectives have sometimes been in tension with it.

Armed forces have historically played a central role in the politics of Latin and Central America and the Caribbean, with numerous military coups, military governments and military-backed authoritarian regimes.[14] When new democratic governments came to power across the region in the 1980s, establishing democratic civil–military relations was a major challenge. Given its position as a long-established democracy and the region's dominant power, the US might have been well placed to support the democratisation of civil–military relations in South America, particularly given its extensive defence diplomacy engagement with the region. History, geopolitics and other competing interests, however, have made US support much more problematic than might be expected. The countries of South America have ambiguous attitudes towards the US and are often wary of its overwhelming power and dominant role. The US itself has a long history of military intervention and support for authoritarian regimes in the region.[15] Defence diplomacy has been an important part of this, with the US cooperating with and providing assistance to the region's militaries despite their involvement in authoritarian rule and human-rights abuses. Policy towards South America has often been controversial in the US and some administrations, notably Jimmy Carter's in the 1970s, have sought to make support for democracy and human rights a central aim, and have ceased military ties with authoritarian regimes.[16] Nevertheless, the dominant historical trend in US defence diplomacy towards South America was the subordination of democracy to other security or economic interests.

Democratisation and the end of the Cold War altered the strategic context for US defence diplomacy towards South America. With the exception of Cuba, all of the countries of South America became democracies – albeit imperfect and often fragile ones. The strategic argument for supporting authoritarian allies against left-wing political forces was mostly, although not entirely, removed, and the promotion of democratic civil–military relations became an explicit and relatively more important goal. The Clinton administration's 1995 *Security Strategy for the Americas* defined one of the 'strategic objectives' of US policy as 'supporting the commitment to democratic norms in the region, including civilian control in defense matters, constructive civil–military relations, and respect for human rights'.[17] At the same time, however, US defence diplomacy towards South America since the 1990s has been shaped by two other new factors. First, the US-led 'war on drugs', initiated by George Bush senior's administration at the end of the 1980s, has become a central element of US policy, resulting in a major increase in military assistance to the Andean countries, in particular Colombia, that are the major source of narcotics entering the US from the region. Second, since September 2001, the US-led 'war on terror' has seen a significant increase in, and redirection of, US military cooperation. The use of defence diplomacy to pursue these two goals is sometimes in tension, if not outright contradiction, with the goal of promoting democratic civil–military relations.

The US maintains extensive defence diplomacy ties with South America.[18] While these activities are managed by the Department of State and/or the Department of Defense, the Southern Command (SOUTHCOM, based at Fort Benning, Georgia) plays a central role in shaping and implementing defence diplomacy towards South America. SOUTHCOM's Commander-in-Chief (CINC) maintains a CINC Initiative Fund and Traditional CINC Activities programme to support military cooperation within the region. The individual US service heads also have Latin American cooperation funds. Each year, approximately 50,000 US military personnel are sent to South America in about 3,000 separate deployments, and each year more than 10,000 South American military personnel are trained by the US. In 1999, then SOUTHCOM CINC General Charles Wilhelm said that 'In the last 12 months I have made 33 trips to the region during which I have made 60 individual country visits'.[19] Most US attention is focused on Argentina, Brazil and Chile (the largest countries in South America), and more recently also Mexico and the Andean states.

US defence diplomacy engagement with South America may be divided into a number of areas:

- **High-level political ties**: US Secretaries of Defense meet bilaterally with their counterparts from the region; Assistant Secretaries of Defense and their staffs maintain regular contacts with their counterparts; there are formal bilateral defence ministry working groups with Argentina, Brazil, Chile, Colombia and Mexico; and the Department of Defense maintains numerous lower-level contacts with defence ministries. These various linkages often provide a framework for the provision of US advice.

- **Military-to-military contacts**: CINC SOUTHCOM maintains numerous contacts with its counterpart militaries in the region; the US Joint Chiefs of Staff also have contacts with their counterparts, including annual bilateral consultations with Argentina, Brazil and Chile; and there are many visits by US military personnel to South America and vice-versa, as well as exchanges between units.

- **Military training and education**: South American military and civilian personnel attend courses at US military training and education facilities; the US sends Military Training Teams (MTTs) and special forces to provide training within the region; the US also maintains a number of institutions specifically to train personnel from South America, including the US Army School of the Americas (renamed the Western Hemisphere Institute for Security Cooperation in 2001), the smaller US Air Force Inter-American Air Forces Academy (IAAFA), the US Navy Small Craft Instruction and Technical Training School (NAVSCIATTS) and the Centre for Hemispheric Defense Studies (CHDS).

- **Joint exercises**: SOUTHCOM organises bilateral and multilateral military exercises with South American militaries (such as the annual UNITAS naval exercise, when a small US task force circumnavigates South America engaging in exercises with the countries of the region[20]); aside from more traditional defence operations, these cover areas such as peacekeeping, humanitarian assistance, disaster relief and counter-narcotics activities. SOUTHCOM also supports a Humanitarian Civic Assistance (HCA) programme, in which US military personnel support the construction of basic infrastructure and the provision of medical services.

- **Arms sales and transfers**: the US government supports the sale or direct transfer of arms to South American states under programmes such as Foreign Military Sales (FMS), Foreign Military Financing (FMF), Direct Commerical Sales (DCS), 'emergency drawdown' and Excess Defence Articles (EDA), as well as more recent counter-narcotics initiatives; a 20-year-old ban on sales of high-technology weapons to the region under FMS, the main programme through which the US government sells arms to other governments, was lifted in 1997.

The promotion of democratic civil–military relations is only one of a variety of objectives behind these various activities. Supporters argue that US defence diplomacy towards South America helps to promote democratic civil–military relations by providing the region's militaries with direct experience of the US model of a democratically and civilian-controlled military, and enhancing their military professionalism.[21] Critics charge that, on top of a history of close cooperation during long periods of authoritarian and military rule, US defence diplomacy reinforces the power and independence of still-powerful militaries and perpetuates patterns of weak or non-existent civilian control.[22]

During the 1990s, the US took a number of steps to redirect its South American defence diplomacy towards supporting democratic civil–military relations. Congress established the E-IMET programme in 1991 specifically for defence management, civil–military relations and military justice. The Department of Defense has used E-IMET to provide courses on these subjects, and to provide training to civilian defence officials.[23]

As part of the reorientation of its defence diplomacy towards democracy and human rights, the US has reformed the Army School of the Americas. The School was established in 1946, and provided training to about 1,000 South American military personnel annually. In the 1980s and 1990s, the School became controversial when it was discovered that its training manuals encouraged counter-insurgency techniques that violated human rights, and that soldiers who had attended it had subsequently committed serious abuses. Pressure grew in Congress for the School to be fundamentally reformed or closed. Congressional amendments to close the School were defeated in 1993 and 1994, but reforms were undertaken, including establishing a Board of Visitors (including independent outside experts) to oversee its activities, and the introduction of a core module on human rights. After continuing pressure, the School was closed in 2000 and reopened the following year as the Western Hemisphere Institute for Security Cooperation. The new Institute is mandated 'to provide professional education and training … within the context of the democratic principles set forth in the Charter of the Organization of American States ... and promoting democratic values, [and] respect for human rights'. The Institute, however, appears likely to remain controversial: although to its supporters the renaming reflects a real commitment to democracy and human rights, to its critics it is little more than window-dressing.[24]

In 1997, the US established the Centre for Hemispheric Defense Studies (CHDS), based at the National Defense University in Washington DC.[25] The CHDS originated in a request from the first inter-American defence ministers' meeting in 1995 for US support in developing civilian defence competence. It is mandated to develop civilian specialists in defence and military matters by providing graduate-level programmes. Between 100 and 200 students participate in CHDS programmes each year, of which about half are civilian government officials, a quarter non-government civilians and a quarter military personnel.

An additional feature of US defence diplomacy since the 1990s has been its multilateralisation in the context of the OAS.[26] Various frameworks for inter-American defence cooperation were established from the Second World War onwards, but these had largely become moribund. After the democratic transitions of the 1980s, interest in inter-American defence dialogue re-emerged. At the initiative of then US Secretary of Defense William Perry, the Western hemisphere's defence ministers met collectively for the first time at Williamsburg, Virginia, in 1995. Since 1996, such meetings have been held biennially. Support for democratic civilian control of armed forces and defence policy has been one of the themes of these meetings. Although this Americas-wide defence dialogue remains relatively limited, it is an additional force for the consolidation of democratic civil–military relations across the region.

US defence diplomacy towards South America has also been shaped by a more powerful dynamic – the 'war on drugs'. The US has provided counter-narcotics military and security assistance to South America, in particular the Andean states. A number of programmes are involved: the State Department's International Narcotics Control (INC) programme, which provides aid to countries where drugs are produced and transported; Department of Defense Section 1004 assistance (which allows the Department to train and transfer equipment to foreign militaries for counter-narcotics purposes) and Section 1033 assistance (which, since 1998, allows it to aid the Colombian and Peruvian security forces in efforts to stem drug smuggling on their waterways); and the Joint Combined Exchange Training (JCET) programme, under which US special forces train overseas with, or provide training to, foreign militaries, including for counter-narcotics purposes. There is also specific congressionally authorised Department of Defense aid to Colombia, Mexico and Peru.[27] The most high-profile element has been Plan Colombia (renamed the Andean Regional Initiative in 2000), under which the US is helping Colombia to counter the left-wing Revolutionary Armed Forces of Colombia (FARC) guerrilla group, which is also involved in the drugs trade. Plan Colombia has made that country the third-largest recipient of US military aid in the world, with the US providing military helicopters and supporting the development of a three-battalion counter-narcotics brigade.[28] This militarised approach to the drugs issue is controversial, and its effectiveness in Colombia and elsewhere remains contentious. In terms of its impact on the democratisation of civil–military relations in the region, however, a number of conclusions may be drawn. For Washington, counter-narcotics military and security assistance is a much higher priority than civil–military relations and has received much more political attention and significantly larger resources. In Colombia and elsewhere in the Andes, counter-narcotics cooperation has involved turning a blind eye to the poor record of the region's militaries on democracy and human rights. At best, US counter-narcotics cooperation does little to support the development of democratic civil–military relations. At worst, it strengthens the region's militaries vis-a-vis civilian governments, reinforces patterns of human-rights abuse and thereby contributes to underlying domestic instability.[29]

The inauguration of the Bush administration and the September 2001 terrorist attacks have reinforced these trends in US policy. The 'war on drugs' and the 'war on terror' now converge in Colombia, with FARC viewed as a threat on both counts. Following the election of President Alvaro Uribe in May 2002, the US has increased military assistance to Colombia as part of Uribe's policy of intensifying military action against FARC. The 'war on terror' has also led to stepped up counter-terrorist cooperation with America's southern neighbours more generally. There are also sometimes tensions within US policy between the goal of supporting democracy in South America and fears that some elected South American governments or leaders, especially of the left, may pose a threat to American interests. US defence diplomacy in the region reflects these tensions. Some within the US, especially on the political right, still view left-wing politicians and movements in South America as a threat to American interests. Against this background, the US appears to have provided tacit backing and limited military support (in communications and intelligence) to right-wingers and elements within the Venezuelan military during their attempt to overthrow the democratically elected president, Hugo Chavez, in April 2002.[30] Although the exact nature of US involvement in the coup attempt remains unclear and there appear to have been divisions within the US government on the issue, the incident sharply illustrates the way in which, especially for the US political right-wing, other perceived interests may run counter to and take priority over the goal of democratising civil–military relations or supporting democracy more generally.[31]

Conclusion

Since the early 1990s, the use of defence diplomacy to support the democratisation of civil–military relations has become an important component of broader Western efforts to promote democracy worldwide. At the same time, the foreign policies of the Western democracies remain shaped by other strategic interests that sometimes lead them to support authoritarian regimes. Even in situations where states have democratised or are democratising, as in South America, tensions may remain. Given these competing interests, the contradiction between support for democracy in some circumstances and cooperation with authoritarian states in others seems likely to remain a feature of Western foreign policies, and defence diplomacy will inevitably reflect this.

The use of defence diplomacy to support the democratisation of civil–military relations is also deeply dependent on both the nature of the regime with which one is engaging and the wider political and strategic environment. Although Western governments sometimes argue that engagement can help to moderate behaviour and even encourage democratic transitions, the evidence suggests that entrenched authoritarian regimes are remarkably resistant to external influence (whether through constructive engagement such as defence diplomacy, or pressure such as political or economic sanctions). The utility of defence diplomacy as a means of influencing civil–military relations in authoritarian regimes is therefore likely to be distinctly limited. States that are reforming, beginning democratic transitions or attempting to consolidate democracy are much more amenable to external influence. In these circumstances, defence diplomacy can be an important means of providing political and practical support for the democratisation of civil–military relations.

The utility of defence diplomacy also depends on the historical, political and strategic circumstances of the countries concerned. The states of post-communist Central and Eastern Europe view themselves as rejoining the West after their artificial separation by the Cold War. Western support has accordingly been actively welcomed, the Western democracies have been seen as a model to be emulated, NATO/PfP has provided a strong institutional framework for cooperation and the prospect of NATO membership has created powerful incentives to implement reform. In contrast, the countries of South America are wary of the United States' hegemonic role within the region, and there has been no equivalent driver for the democratisation of civil–military relations. Given their experience of Western imperialism, intervention and support for authoritarian regimes, many countries in Africa, Asia and the Middle East are similarly wary of Western attempts at defence diplomacy, often viewing it as a cover for the promotion of strategic or economic interests, and so resist or at best reluctantly accept it.

A further problem is the military-to-military character of much defence diplomacy. While cooperation with Western militaries may help to spread norms of democratic civilian control and professionalism, it also risks ignoring other dimensions of the problem (such as the need for parliamentary oversight and civil society engagement with defence issues). Western governments have sought to address this problem by increasing the training available to civilians and encouraging civil–military interaction in defence diplomacy activities. More could and should be done, in particular with regard to parliamentary oversight, the rule of law, respect for human rights and civil society engagement.

Although the 'war on terror' is reshaping Western, especially US, defence diplomacy, the promotion of democratic civil–military relations, and of democracy more generally, remain long-term goals of Western policy, even if the priority attached to them has been lowered. At the same time, the 'war on terror' has created new situations in which defence diplomacy is being used to support the democratisation of civil–military relations. In both Afghanistan and

Iraq, Western governments are backing attempts to establish reformed, democratically controlled armed forces as part of wider efforts at stabilisation and democratisation. The 'war on terror' has also provoked wider debate on Western support for authoritarian regimes: some (including influential neo-conservatives within the Bush administration) argue that a key underlying cause of radical Islamic terrorism has been the absence of democracy in the Middle East and the West's support for authoritarian regimes in countries such as Saudi Arabia and Egypt, with the implication that such support should be abandoned. While the September 2001 attacks have in the short term led to closer military cooperation with a number of authoritarian regimes, the longer-term impact on Western attitudes to democracy and authoritarianism elsewhere in the world and on Western defence diplomacy remain to be seen.

Chapter 3

Enhancing Regional Peacekeeping Capabilities

The third new purpose to which Western states have put defence diplomacy since the 1990s is supporting partner countries in developing peacekeeping capabilities. In post-communist Europe, Africa and elsewhere, the leading Western democracies have sought to encourage other states to contribute to peacekeeping operations, and have used defence diplomacy as a means of supporting them in developing the required military capabilities.

Since the mid-1980s, there has been a major increase in demand for peacekeeping operations, with the UN, regional organisations and ad hoc coalitions undertaking a large number of new operations. There has also been a shift away from traditional UN peacekeeping – which essentially monitored ceasefires – and towards a variety of more demanding peace enforcement operations, where force has been used to impose a peace, and post-conflict operations involving a wide range of peace-building tasks (such as monitoring elections and human rights, disarming and demobilising combatants and supporting social and economic reconstruction). As a result, many of the operations initiated over the last two decades have been significantly larger than before, and have placed much greater demands on participating militaries. Many have also resulted in long-term, indeed often open-ended, commitments of significant numbers of soldiers. At the same time states, especially the Western states with the most capacity to act, have become reluctant to commit troops to risky humanitarian interventions where immediate national interests are not involved – as illustrated most starkly by the failure of the international community and especially the major Western powers to intervene in the Rwandan genocide in 1994.

All of these factors resulted in growing pressure for non-Western states and regional organisations to contribute more to international peacekeeping. During the 1990s, regional and sub-regional organisations such as NATO, the European Union (EU), the Organisation of African Unity (OAU, renamed the African Union in 2002) and the Economic Community of West African States (ECOWAS) embraced peacekeeping as within their remit, and took steps to develop the capacity to undertake peacekeeping operations. Western governments, in particular the US, the UK and France, also initiated programmes to support regional organisations and their members in developing peacekeeping capabilities.

As with other elements of the new defence diplomacy, the attempt to support partners in developing their peacekeeping capabilities is not new, but it does represent a significant shift in patterns of military cooperation and assistance. Helping partner states to strengthen their armed forces has long been a goal of old-style defence diplomacy. In the past, this was generally directed against a specific common external or internal enemy; did not have wider goals; and usually took little cognisance of human-rights concerns. In contrast, efforts to enhance regional peacekeeping capabilities since the 1990s have not been directed against specific external enemies, but rather towards the general problem of peacekeeping; have been part of the wider goal of promoting regional cooperation and confidence-building; and take place in the context of more general efforts to promote democracy, good governance and human rights. This chapter analyses the role of Western defence diplomacy assistance in supporting partners to develop peacekeeping capabilities, examining the role of NATO and the EU in Central and Eastern Europe and a number of initiatives in Africa, and drawing wider conclusions about its utility, its limits and the dilemmas it presents.

NATO and the EU: enhancing peacekeeping capabilities in the Euro-Atlantic region

As part of their wider policies of outreach and integration in post-communist Europe, NATO, and to a lesser extent the EU, have encouraged the countries of the region to contribute to peacekeeping missions, and have sought to support them in developing the required military capabilities. Cooperation in peacekeeping became a key element of the PfP, and contributing to such missions a prerequisite for aspiring NATO members. When the PfP was established in 1994, its goals included the 'maintenance of the capability and readiness to contribute' to peacekeeping operations and the development of military cooperation in order to undertake peacekeeping, search and rescue, humanitarian and other missions.[1] NATO's operations in Bosnia, Kosovo and Macedonia became key drivers for the development of Central and Eastern Europe contributions to peacekeeping.

NATO/PfP cooperation on peacekeeping has a number of dimensions:

- NATO and the PfP have been key frameworks for efforts to develop common peacekeeping concepts and operational doctrines as a basis for cooperation in peacekeeping in the field. This resulted in a series of commonly-agreed reports, including a 1993 North Atlantic Cooperation Council (NACC) report on cooperation, a 1995 *Compendium of Lessons Learned in Peacekeeping Operations* and a 1999 *Compendium of Views and Experiences on the Humanitarian Aspects of Peacekeeping.*[2] SHAPE has also developed a generic set of crisis-management documents: the *Generic Crisis Management Handbook*, the *Inventory of Preventive Measures*, the *Generic Catalogue of Military Response Options* and the *Generic Manual of Precautionary Measures*. This conceptual and doctrinal work has laid the basis for NATO and its PfP partners to work alongside each other in peacekeeping operations, primarily in the former Yugoslavia. Early hopes of a Europe-wide peacekeeping doctrine, however, proved optimistic. Significant differences in national approaches to peacekeeping and especially peace enforcement remain, both within NATO and between NATO and its PfP partners. Furthermore, tensions with Russia over NATO's intervention in Kosovo illustrated that conceptual and doctrinal discussions cannot overcome fundamental political questions over the rights and wrongs of intervention.

- Through the Partnership Coordination Cell, NATO has provided the institutional framework for integrating PfP partners and other non-members into its peacekeeping operations, in particular through the planning of joint military exercises. NATO's peacekeeping operations in former Yugoslavia led to the creation of an International Coordination Centre to provide briefing and planning facilities for all non-NATO countries contributing forces to NATO-led missions. Partners have participated in planning and force generation processes.

- Peacekeeping and related tasks have been a core part of the multilateral military exercises that are a central element of the PfP. The first PfP exercise was held in September 1994 in Poland, bringing together forces from six NATO states and seven partner states to train for peacekeeping.[3] PfP crisis-management exercises began in 1995, and have been held annually since 1998.

- NATO offers direct support to PfP partners for the development of national peacekeeping capabilities. NATO experts advise partner states on the development of peacekeeping forces and crisis-management capabilities. In 1999, NATO established a PfP Training Education Enhancement Programme and PfP Training Centres (national facilities offering training to PfP partners and supported by NATO expertise and assistance).[4] Five PfP Training Centres have been established, in Turkey, Ukraine, Switzerland, Romania and Sweden. Although these centres offer training in other areas, peacekeeping is a core focus. Most NATO members, and some PfP partners such as Finland and Sweden, also provide bilateral peacekeeping assistance to Central and Eastern European states and support multilateral peacekeeping projects. Examples of the latter include Nordic support for Latvia, Lithuania and Estonia's joint Baltic Battalion peacekeeping force, and the Danish-led ten-country Baltic Defence College in Estonia. Canada provides peacekeeping training to Central and Eastern European states through the Peace Training Support Centre and the Lester B. Pearson Peacekeeping Centre in Nova Scotia.[5]

- NATO's enlargement into Central and Eastern Europe also became a key driver for the development of peacekeeping and power-projection capabilities, with the Alliance making clear to aspirants that the ability to contribute to such operations was a prerequisite of membership. Within this context, the various PfP institutions, in particular the PARP and the MAP, provided a framework for discussing reform, providing advice and making recommendations to aspirants.

Although NATO has played the primary role in supporting the development of peacekeeping capacity in Central and Eastern Europe, the EU and the Western European Union (WEU) – the EU's military crisis-management arm until it took on this role directly in 1999 – have also had a part in this area.[6] During the 1990s, the WEU undertook a number of small crisis-management operations, including enforcing economic sanctions against Yugoslavia in the Adriatic Sea and on the Danube River and supporting Albania in developing its police force. WEU partnership arrangements with Central and Eastern European states included discussions on peacekeeping, and small Central and Eastern European contributions were integrated into its operations. New structures have been established to integrate these states into the EU's emerging defence policy following the Union's decision in 1999 to develop a defence role, and these countries have offered contributions towards the EU's projected 60,000-strong rapid reaction force.

In terms of the impact of defence diplomacy in enhancing Central and Eastern European peacekeeping capabilities, the evidence is mixed. As Table 3.1 illustrates, Poland, the Czech Republic, Slovakia, Hungary and Romania, which to various degrees had already contributed to UN operations, have increased their contributions to peacekeeping since the early 1990s. The Baltic states and Slovenia have become active contributors to peacekeeping operations, albeit on a small scale. Russia and Ukraine have made large contributions to peacekeeping, in particular to the NATO-led operations in Bosnia and Kosovo. A number of Central and Eastern European states have contributed forces to the International Security Assistance Force (ISAF) in Afghanistan and the post-war US operation in Iraq. Overall, there has been a significant but not dramatic increase in the ability of Central and Eastern European states to contribute to peacekeeping operations. In terms of contributions to UN peacekeeping operations, Table 3.2 shows that Central and Eastern European states contributed about 15% of total UN forces at the end of 2003. Nor has integrating Central and Eastern European forces into these various peacekeeping missions proved

Table 3.1:	**Central and Eastern European contributions to peacekeeping, 1992 and 2002**			
	Total active military personnel 1992	Personnel engaged in peacekeeping 1992	Total active military personnel 2002	Personnel engaged in peacekeeping 2002
Bulgaria	107,000	474	68,450	8
Czechoslovakia	145,800	524	–	–
Czech Republic	–	–	49,450	775
Estonia	2,000	–	5,150	3
Hungary	80,800	24	33,400	655
Latvia	2,550	–	5,500	112
Lithuania	7,000	–	13,510	125
Poland	296,500	1,327	163,000	1,808
Romania	200,000	7	99,200	905
Russia	2,720,000	1031	977,100	7,125
Slovakia	–	–	26,200	641
Slovenia	15,000	–	9,000	86
Ukraine	230,000	900	302,300	1,629

Source: *The Military Balance 1992–1993* (London: Brassey's for the IISS, 1992); and *The Military Balance 2002–2003* (Oxford: Oxford University Press for the IISS, 2002).

Table 3.2:	**Central and Eastern European contributions to UN peacekeeping operations (December 2003)**			
	Civilian Police	Military Observers	Troops	Total
Bulgaria	82	6	2	90
Czech Republic	16	21	1	38
Estonia	-	2	-	2
Hungary	7	15	120	142
Latvia	-	-	-	-
Lithuania	8	-	-	8
Poland	124	19	592	735
Romania	176	42	1	219
Russia	121	87	115	323
Slovakia	-	4	493	497
Slovenia	13	2	-	15
Ukraine	194	33	834	1,061
CEE total	741	231	2,158	3,130
Overall total of UN forces	4,635	1,851	39,329	45,815

Source: *Contributors to United Nations Peacekeeping Operations (as of 31 December 2003), UN website, http://www.un.org/Depts/dpko/dpko/contributors/December2003Countrysummary.pdf*

especially problematic. By creating political pressure to contribute, providing advice on capabilities and preparing states for functional integration, Western defence diplomacy has thus been reasonably successful in enhancing the Central and Eastern European contribution to peacekeeping.

Nevertheless, there remain significant limitations to the Central and Eastern European states' ability to contribute to peacekeeping operations. In general, they lack the capacity to deploy rapidly, or the ability to contribute greatly (if at all) to enforcement tasks at the more challenging end of the spectrum of conflict. As a consequence, while they are able to contribute to traditional peacekeeping tasks and work alongside the US and major Western European militaries, they cannot replace the core roles performed by the latter in peace enforcement operations such as those in Bosnia, Kosovo and Afghanistan. During NATO's 1999 war in Kosovo, for example, Central and Eastern European countries were unable to contribute air forces and Hungary required US support in patrolling its airspace.[7] Similarly, when the ISAF was established in Afghanistan at the beginning of 2002, long-standing EU members, led by the UK, provided 80% of forces, with only Bulgaria and Romania from Central and Eastern Europe providing forces on the ground (and then only in small numbers, ten and 40 soldiers respectively).[8]

The Central and Eastern European states are taking steps to enhance their contribution to traditional peacekeeping missions, and to develop more rapidly deployable power-projection forces capable of contributing to peace enforcement operations.[9] This shift has progressed furthest in the three states that joined NATO in 1999 (Poland, the Czech Republic and Hungary), but is also visible in the seven countries invited to join the Alliance in 2002. In September 2001, the Czech government announced that it would abolish conscription by 2007, and other states appear likely to move in a similar direction.[10] In a significant step, in 2003 the US decided to place a sector of post-war Iraq under Polish command (although the Polish forces require significant US support to enable them to fulfil this role).

NATO and the EU have been key drivers behind the effort by Central and Eastern European states to develop peacekeeping and power-projection capabilities, and Western defence diplomacy has been central to operationalising this. Critics argue that there are tensions between the development of power-projection forces and the maintenance of a territorial defence capacity, since focusing on the former may undermine the latter. Once states join NATO and the EU, political pressure to devote scarce resources to defence reforms may decline – as was arguably the case in Poland, the Czech Republic and Hungary. The continuing demand for peacekeeping and intervention, the centrality of this to NATO and the EU, and the low likelihood of traditional military threats to territorial integrity, however, will probably continue to drive the Central and Eastern European states towards the development of peacekeeping and power-projection forces – but this will be a slow process.

'African solutions for African problems': building regional peacekeeping capacity

Since the early 1990s, there have been growing efforts to strengthen Africa's ability to deal with its security problems by developing regional conflict prevention, management and resolution capabilities. This reflects both the reluctance of external powers, especially the major Western powers, to intervene in African conflicts, and a desire within Africa to assert the continent's independence. One element of this regional approach to security-building has been an effort to develop regional peacekeeping capabilities. Western governments, in particular the US, the UK and France, have used defence diplomacy as a key means of trying to strengthen African states' peacekeeping capabilities. These efforts are complemented by greater Western interest in promoting democratic civil–military relations, military respect for human rights and the responsible management of defence. They therefore mark a broader shift in Western military engagement with Africa.

The failure of the international community to intervene in the 1994 Rwandan genocide was a key driver behind efforts to enhance regional peacekeeping capacity. In 1995, the UN Secretary-General Boutros Boutros-Ghali published a report calling for international efforts to help develop African peacekeeping capabilities. In 1996, fears of a Rwanda-style bloodbath in Burundi led the US to propose a new multinational African Crisis Response Force (ACRF). This was criticised on the grounds that what was needed was not a new force, but rather enhancing the ability of states' existing armed forces, and in response the African Crisis Response Initiative (ACRI) was established to provide peacekeeping training for African states. At the same time, France developed the RECAMP (Renforcement des capacités africaines de maintien de la paix) initiative and the UK an African Peacekeeping Training Support Programme. In May 1997, the three countries launched the so-called P3 Initiative, a common peacekeeping capacity-building programme. When British Prime Minister Tony Blair and French President Jacques Chiraq launched proposals for an EU defence role at their St. Malo summit in December 1998, they also committed themselves to coordinating policies towards Africa, including support for African states in developing peacekeeping capacity. Other countries, in particular the Nordic states and Canada, are also supporting the development of African peacekeeping capabilities. In December 1997, the UN hosted the first of a series of meetings on enhancing Africa's peacekeeping capacity. The Group of Eight (G-8) states have endorsed these various initiatives, and act as a further coordinating mechanism.

Western defence diplomacy support for the development of African peacekeeping has taken a number of forms:

- **Peacekeeping training and education**: between 1996 and 2002, the US ACRI programme provided peacekeeping training to over 8,600 troops from Senegal, Uganda, Malawi, Mali, Ghana, Benin, Côte d'Ivoire and Kenya. ACRI training was conducted in Africa by US special forces soldiers, focused on units up to battalion level, and aimed to train between ten and 14 battalions. It was based around a series of modules covering areas relevant to peacekeeping, culminating in an 8–10-day field training exercise. In 2002, the Bush administration replaced ACRI with the Africa Contingency Training Assistance (ACOTA) programme, which trains troops for peace-enforcement operations and provides them with offensive military equipment.[11] Whereas the US has focused on training full units, the UK's African Peacekeeping Training Support Programme aims to train officers, who will in turn train troops within their own countries. There are three British Military Advisory and Training Teams (BMATTs) – BMATT West Africa (based in Ghana), BMATT Southern Africa (originally based in Zimbabwe) and BMATT East Africa (based in Uganda). The UK also has British Military Liaison Officers (BMLOs) based in Angola, Ethiopia and Mauritius, and sends

Short-Term Training Teams (STTTs) to Africa, both of which play a smaller role in supporting the development of peacekeeping capacity. France has helped to establish a regional peacekeeping training centre in Côte d'Ivoire, and pays the costs of officers from West African states attending its courses. France also provides financial assistance and instructors to national military staff colleges in Côte d'Ivoire, Mali, Mauritania, Senegal and Togo, where training includes a peacekeeping component. Denmark has funded a Regional Peacekeeping Training Centre in Zimbabwe's Staff College, as well as organising visits by Southern African Development Community (SADC) ministers and officials to Europe to learn about Nordic and Baltic experiences in peacekeeping.

- **Multilateral peacekeeping exercises**: the French RECAMP programme aims to use multilateral exercises as a means of developing sub-regional Stand-by Force Modules that can then be deployed in peacekeeping operations. The first RECAMP exercise took place in Togo in March 1997. The second, called *Guidimakha*, was held in Senegal in February 1998, and brought together 3,600 soldiers from eight African countries, France, the UK and the US. France plans to continue to support such exercises every two years, but on cost grounds will limit their size to roughly 1,000 participants. The UK has also supported exercises as a means of enhancing peacekeeping capabilities. In April 1997, the UK supported and helped to organise (at a cost of over $500,000) a three-week peacekeeping exercise, *Blue Hungwe*, in Zimbabwe, which brought together more than 1,500 troops from ten SADC countries, as well as British and other Western soldiers. Under the FLINTLOCK programme, the US has sponsored regional military exercises in Africa, in some of which peacekeeping has been the focus. Other Western states, again in particular the Nordic countries and Canada, have contributed on a smaller scale.
- **Providing equipment to African states for peacekeeping operations**: the pre-positioning of equipment in African states is a key part of the French RECAMP programme. The equipment will remain under French control, but will be loaned to African states participating in exercises and actual peacekeeping operations. Equipment pre-positioned as part of

the *Guidimakha* exercise was subsequently used to support the UN peacekeeping force in the Central African Republic. As part of the ACRI, the US provides each participating African state with approximately $1.2m-worth of equipment, again for use in exercises and peacekeeping operations. The UK's African Peacekeeping Training Support Programme does not, in general, involve the provision of equipment. The US, the UK, France and other Western countries have provided equipment and material support for specific peacekeeping operations, such as the ECOMOG operation in Liberia and the UN mission in Sierra Leone. In general, Western states have provided only non-lethal equipment, focusing on areas such as transport, communications, mine detectors and basic items like uniforms.

The impact of these efforts to support the development of African peacekeeping capabilities has been limited. There has certainly been no dramatic increase in the ability or willingness of African states to contribute to peacekeeping since the early 1990s. As Table 3.3 illustrates, the majority of African countries contribute very little to international peacekeeping forces (whether in Africa or elsewhere). Even states which make sizable contributions, such as Ghana, Guinea, Kenya, Morocco, Nigeria, Senegal, Tunisia and Zambia, have not greatly increased their participation since the early 1990s. The largest African contribution to peacekeeping has been Nigeria's in West Africa, where it has direct interests. The ability of the various peacekeeping forces deployed in Africa since the mid-1990s to bring peace to the continent's many war-torn countries has also been, at best, limited. The UN mission deployed to support a peace agreement in Angola in 1995 (UNAVEM II) withdrew in 1997 when fighting was renewed. The UN Mission in Congo (MONUC), deployed to support a peace agreement in 2001, has only 3,500 troops, far too few to police the fragile ceasefire in one of Africa's largest countries. The largest peacekeeping force currently deployed in Africa is the UN mission in Sierra Leone (UNAMSIL), with just over 11,500 troops in total (see Table 3.4). African states supply over a third of these soldiers – a major contribution, but hardly indicative of an ability to act without significant outside participation and support. When UNAMSIL's peacekeeping efforts appeared on the verge of collapse in 2000, it was Britain – the old imperial power – that undertook more forceful

Table 3.3: **African contributions to peacekeeping, 1992 and 2002**

	Total active military personnel 1992	Personnel engaged in peacekeeping 1992	Total active military personnel 2002	Personnel engaged in peacekeeping 2002
Algeria	139,000	34	124,000	21
Angola	127,500	–	130,500	–
Benin	4,350	–	4,750	–
Botswana	6,100	–	9,000	–
Burkina Faso	8,700	–	10,000	10
Burundi	7,200	–	45,500	–
Cameroon	11,700	–	22,100	–
Cape Verdi	1,300	–	1,200	–
Central African Republic	6,500	–	4,150	–
Chad	25,200	–	30,350	–
Congo	10,850	15	10,000	–
Côte d'Ivoire	7,100	–	13,900	–
DRC/Zaire	54,100	–	81,400	–
Djibouti	3,800	–	9,600	–
Egypt	410,000	27	443,000	134
Equatorial Guinea	1,300	–	1,320	–
Eritrea	–	–	171,900	–
Ethiopia	110,000	–	252,500	–
Gabon	4,750	–	4,700	–
Gambia	800	100	800	30
Ghana	7,200	2,672	7,000	1,693
Guinea	9,700	402	9,700	792
Guinea-Bissau	9,200	15	9,250	–
Kenya	24,200	56	24,400	2,016
Lesotho	2,000	–	2,000	–
Liberia	5,000	–	11–15,000	–
Madagascar	21,000	–	13,500	–
Malawi	10,750	–	5,300	17
Mali	7,350	–	7,350	9
Mauritania	9,600	–	15,650	–
Mauritius	–	–	1,600*	–
Morocco	195,500	14	198,500	1,697
Mozambique	50,200	–	10,600–11,600	14
Namibia	7,500	–	9,000	5
Niger	3,300	–	5,300	13
Nigeria	76,000	4,892	78,500	3,307
Rwanda	5,200	–	56–71,000	–
Senegal	9,700	1,224	9,400–10,000	560
Seychelles	1,300	–	450	–
Sierra Leone	6,150	400	6,000	–
Somalia	–	–	–	–
South Africa	72,400	–	61,500	114
Sudan	82,500	–	117,000	–
Tanzania	46,800	–	27,000	27
Togo	5,250	–	9,450	–
Tunisia	35,000	435	35,000	249
Uganda	70–100,000	–	50–60,000	–
Zambia	24,000	–	21,600	859
Zimbabwe	48,500	15	39,000	–

* Paramilitary forces

Sources: *The Military Balance 1992–93* (London: Brassey's for the IISS, 1992); *The Military Balance 2002–03* (Oxford: Oxford University Press for the IISS, 2002).

Table 3.4: **African contributions to UNAMSIL in Sierra Leone, (December 2003)**			
Troops (inc. military observers, staff officers and headquarters staff)			
African Contributions		**Other Contributions**	
Egypt	10	Bangladesh	1,503
Gambia	15	Nepal	814
Ghana	793	Pakistan	3,865
Guinea	13	Ukraine	645
Kenya	1,014	Others *	378
Mali	5	**Total other contributions**	7,205
Nigeria	1,627		
Tanzania	12		
Zambia	834		
Total Africa contributions	4,323	**Overall force size**	11,528

* Smaller numbers of troops contributed by: Bolivia, Canada, China, Croatia, Czech Republic, Denmark, Germany, Indonesia, Jordan, Kyrgyzstan, Malaysia, New Zealand, Russia, Slovakia, Sweden, Thailand, United Kingdom and Uruguay.

Source: Twentieth report of the Secretary-General on the United Nations Mission in Sierra Leone (UNAMSIL), UN Security Council, S/2003/1201, 23 December 2003.

intervention to stabilise the situation. The largest African contributor to peacekeeping missions, Nigeria, has also become increasingly reluctant to dedicate forces, and has withdrawn troops from some missions. Indeed, Nigeria's withdrawal of the majority of its 12,000 forces from the earlier ECOMOG force in Liberia and Sierra Leone contributed directly to the near-collapse of the UNAMSIL mission in 2000 and the instability that led Nigeria to send forces back into Liberia in 2003.

With the transition from apartheid to democracy, some observers hoped that South Africa, the continent's largest and most populous country, might play a leading role in peacekeeping. Although South Africa's armed forces are probably amongst the most capable within Africa and the country has begun to participate in peacekeeping operations, the development of this role has been slow. Having had almost no soldiers involved in peacekeeping in the 1990s, since 2000 South Africa has deployed 3,000 peacekeepers in Africa, primarily in Burundi and Congo.[12] South Africa also lacks the ability to project and sustain its armed forces on a significant scale beyond its borders. The armed forces routinely work with the police in providing military aid to civilian authorities inside the country, a National Office for the Co-ordination of Peace Missions has been established, and since 1999 peacekeeping has been on the curriculum of Army and Joint Staff courses. However, South Africa is unlikely on its own to be able to resolve the continent's peacekeeping problems.

The limited impact of the various external efforts to enhance African peacekeeping capabilities is explained by a number of factors. While there is general support for the approach, the attempt to develop 'African solutions for African problems' – specifically how and implemented by whom – is highly problematic.[13] Africans fear that Western support for the development of African peacekeeping capacity is simply political cover for the West's reluctance to intervene in African conflicts, while also allowing the West to continue to impose its agenda. US Department of Defense officials reportedly acknowledged that the initial proposal for an African Crisis Response Force was 'total bullshit, and we knew it from day one'.[14] African concerns over Western peacekeeping support initiatives led Nigeria's Foreign Minister to denounce them at an OAU Council of Ministers meeting in March 1998, reportedly with the support of Kenya, South Africa and Zimbabwe. Two of Africa's leading states, Egypt and South Africa, refused to accept ACRI training.[15] Continuing African distrust of Western motives will not easily be overcome.

The gap between the capabilities necessary for effective peacekeeping and the realities of most African armed forces is also great. African militaries are poorly equipped, training is limited and many lack the professional standards of their Western counterparts. As Eric Berman and Katie Sams observe: 'OAU Member States remain crippled by scant economic resources and inadequate military infrastructures to mount operations beyond their borders'.[16] Although ECOWAS has been able to deploy forces, corruption, human rights violations, poor leadership and low morale hampered its operations in Sierra Leone and Liberia.[17] A 1996 audit concluded that only eight African states (Botswana, Ethiopia, Ghana, Kenya, Nigeria, Senegal, South Africa and Zimbabwe) could meet the minimum standards necessary for peacekeeping.[18] Although the African Union and sub-regional groups such as SADC and ECOWAS have adopted peacekeeping as part of their agenda, their ability to actually mount operations remains severely limited.[19] In particular, they lack the institutions necessary for the command and control of peacekeeping operations and common doctrines for the conduct of such operations, and progress in remedying these deficiencies is slow.

African states and their Western partners have also been reluctant to address the issue of peace enforcement, as distinct from traditional peacekeeping. African states remain deeply wary of external intervention in their affairs, and are strongly attached to the principle of state sovereignty. OAU Chiefs of Staff have explicitly ruled out any OAU (now African Union) involvement in peace-enforcement operations.[20] The programmes established in the mid-1990s focused on traditional UN-style peacekeeping, with its basis in the consent of the parties to the conflict.[21] The relatively low-risk nature of traditional peacekeeping has meant that both African and Western states have been willing to supply forces for such missions in Africa. In contrast, both Western and African states have been reluctant to deploy forces in more dangerous situations, where elements of peace enforcement may be necessary. UN operations of this type have failed to achieve agreed force levels and have often been ineffective, notably in Rwanda in 1993–94, Sierra Leone and the Democratic Republic of Congo (DRC). African militaries also lack the equipment necessary for peace enforcement operations, especially strategic transport aircraft, tactical transport and ground equipment (helicopters and armoured personnel carriers).[22] Since the late 1990s, these problems have been recognised and Western assistance programmes are now beginning to provide both training and equipment for more offensive operations, as indicated by the US shift from ACRI to ACOTA.

Given these problems, the development of African peacekeeping capabilities is likely to be a slow process, and the ability of African states to provide solutions to the continent's peacekeeping problems is likely to remain limited. Building up African peacekeeping capabilities via defence diplomacy can only be regarded as a long-term project. Defence diplomacy assistance for the development of peacekeeping capabilities will also remain vulnerable to wider political relations. Zimbabwe, for example, was viewed in the mid-1990s by the West as one of the main potential partners in this area, but the growing authoritarianism of Robert Mugabe's regime and the subsequent political crisis in the country have ended hopes of such a role. Nor is defence diplomacy risk-free. Armed forces and civil–military relations are an important part of the wider problems of weak states, democratisation and human-rights abuse in Africa. Enhancing African armed forces' military capabilities risks strengthening them politically, and there is the possibility that training and equipment may be abused for purposes of internal repression or external aggression. Defence diplomacy assistance for the development of African peacekeeping capabilities should therefore be viewed as only one part, and often not the most central element, of the much larger challenge of state-building and democratisation on the continent.[23] One positive sign is that since the OAU became the African Union in 2002 agreement has been reached on the establishment of an African Security Council (modelled on the UN Security Council) and five brigades of soldiers, police and military observers – totalling 15,000 personnel – for peacekeeping operations.[24] The effectiveness of these forces, however, remains to be seen and external defence diplomacy type support is likely to be important to their on-going development.

Conclusion

The cases examined here illustrate both the potential and the limitations and problems of the use of defence diplomacy to help partners develop their peacekeeping capacity. Central and Eastern European states have increased their contributions to peacekeeping since the early 1990s. While the various initiatives in Africa have made only limited progress, their success or failure should be judged over the longer term. Nevertheless, most small and medium-sized states can make only limited contributions to peacekeeping. In Europe, leading Western states have provided the core of the NATO-led peacekeeping forces into which Central and Eastern European contributions have been integrated. The US played the same role in Haiti in the mid-1990s, as did Australia in East Timor at the end of the decade. In contrast, in Africa the reluctance of Western states to intervene has meant that there has generally been no core of capable armed forces with which African contributions might be integrated. The wider regional political and strategic environment also has an important bearing on the prospects for using defence diplomacy to develop peacekeeping capacity. In Europe, NATO and the EU have provided a vital political and military framework, and the majority of Central and Eastern European states are supportive. Elsewhere in the world, regional organisations – despite rhetorical commitments to peacekeeping – do not play such a central role, peacekeeping is often seen as a threat to state sovereignty, governments are wary of the imposition of Western agendas and there are fewer incentives for states to contribute forces.

A number of steps might be taken to address some of these problems. First, larger states could be encouraged to contribute to peacekeeping on a much more significant scale than currently, especially outside their own regions. Countries such as Germany, Japan, India, Argentina, Brazil, China and Iran have the potential to make a much larger contribution than smaller Central and Eastern European and African states. Western defence diplomacy could prioritise relations with these countries and focus on peacekeeping as a key area in these relationships; such an approach could also be linked to UN Security Council reform, with permanent membership a prospect in return for a significantly greater contribution to international security. Western defence diplomacy engagement with these states on peacekeeping would also have the wider benefit of building cooperative relations more broadly.

Second, the NATO/PfP model, whereby Western states provide a peacekeeping/enforcement core into which other contributions can be integrated, could be expanded beyond Europe. This might be done in a number of ways: by establishing a framework similar to NATO's PfP for cooperation between NATO and partners beyond Europe; through the EU's emerging defence role, which might act as a pole of attraction to build partnership relationships with other regional organisations (such as the African Union); via bilateral links with states that already have a relationship with the EU; and by encouraging joint peacekeeping training and exercises between Western states and other partners, with the prospect of meaningful engagement with NATO, the EU and leading Western powers (which could provide an additional incentive for participation).

Bringing a wider group of states into international peacekeeping and enforcement will not allow Western governments to avoid difficult dilemmas about whether, when and how to intervene in conflicts, at least in the medium term. Nevertheless, some modest successes have been achieved, particularly in Central and Eastern Europe, and there are strong arguments for expanding peacekeeping capabilities beyond the West. More equitable sharing of the burden of maintaining international peace and security is a desirable goal in itself. It will also strengthen the legitimacy of peacekeeping as a whole and may, in the longer term, contribute to the development of a wider consensus on sensitive questions of peace enforcement and intervention. Engagement on peacekeeping may also have positive benefits in terms of building cooperative relations with the states involved. Further progress will, however, require active and sustained engagement with a wider range of large powers, and greater use of core Western capabilities as a framework. In parallel, there will also need to be more attention to the political conditionality of the defence diplomacy on offer, if Western governments are to hold true to their commitment not only to the development of peacekeeping capabilities, but also to the promotion of democracy, good governance and human rights.

Conclusion

Over the last decade there have been major changes in patterns of international defence diplomacy. Historically, defence diplomacy – military cooperation and assistance – has been used for realpolitik purposes of strengthening allies against common enemies. Since the early 1990s, there has been a shift on the part of Western governments towards the use of defence diplomacy for a range of new purposes. These include military cooperation with former or potential enemies as part of wider attempts to improve relations with these states; support for multilateral regional military cooperation as a tool of conflict prevention; support for the democratisation of civil–military relations and security sector reform more generally; support for countries attempting to rebuild or reform their armed forces after conflict or political transition; and support for the development of regional peacekeeping capabilities. This paper describes this change in patterns of international military cooperation and assistance as a shift from 'old' to 'new' forms of defence diplomacy. Two defining features distinguish the new defence diplomacy from the old: first, it is directed primarily towards promoting cooperation among the states involved, rather than against an external enemy; and second, it is centrally concerned with the internal governance of the states in question, in particular the promotion of democratic civil–military relations, good governance of the security sector and respect for human rights.

The expansion of the goals of Western defence diplomacy has reshaped military cooperation and assistance programmes. Western governments are now pursuing military cooperation with a much wider range of partners than in the past, including potential adversaries and states undergoing difficult internal transitions. The aim of defence diplomacy in these circumstances is to help turn adversaries into partners, and to influence domestic transitions in positive directions. Western governments are now also engaged in a much wider range of military cooperation than in the past. Existing activities and programmes have been restructured, and new ones introduced. The promotion of democratic civilian control of armed forces and liberal democratic values more generally has also become more central to Western defence diplomacy. The combined effect differentiates current Western defence diplomacy from that of the past.

The new defence diplomacy, however, continues to run alongside the old, and there are tensions between the two. For many states and in many regions of the world, defence diplomacy remains primarily about the realpolitik goal of supporting allies against perceived enemies. The Western democracies that have been the primary architects of the new defence diplomacy also continue to use defence diplomacy to support allies against common enemies, despite the poor records of some of those allies on democracy and human rights. In the wake of the September 2001 attacks, there has been a shift back towards old defence diplomacy, with the US and other Western governments providing new counter-terrorist military assistance to a number of authoritarian regimes and countries with poor human-rights records.

The interaction between new and old defence diplomacy has resulted in the emergence of distinctive patterns of military cooperation with different partners and in different regions. Defence diplomacy cooperation amongst the established democracies, primarily within NATO and the US alliances with Australia, New Zealand, Japan and South Korea, is underpinned by shared threats and common values. Although the goal of military cooperation between these states has shifted from countering the Soviet Union to new missions such as peacekeeping and counter-terrorism, the underlying pattern of extensive defence cooperation designed to enhance the collective ability to deal with common threats has not changed. Here, the old defence diplomacy goals are compatible with the newer goals of promoting democracy and overcoming historical enmities. Indeed, while post-Second World War defence cooperation was established in the first place to deal with common external threats, it also played a central role in helping to reintegrate Germany and Japan into the community of democracies.

A second pattern of defence diplomacy is that between the Western democracies and what may be described as allies of convenience. This includes both longstanding military cooperation relationships, such as those between Western states and Saudi Arabia, Egypt and Pakistan, and newer relationships in the context of the US-led 'war on terrorism', such as those with the Central Asian countries. Defence diplomacy cooperation in these relationships is based on shared but limited strategic interests, such as containing particular states and countering terrorism, but not on broader common values; it therefore often involves the West ignoring the authoritarian nature and human-rights abuses of partner regimes. While the end of the Cold War removed one key rationale for such military cooperation, others – regional threats such as Iran and Iraq, maintaining access to oil resources and counter-terrorism – remain. From the perspective of the Western democracies, while defence diplomacy cooperation with allies of convenience may help in addressing some key security challenges, it is also deeply problematic. It runs counter to Western commitments to democracy and human rights, and undermines broader efforts to support these goals. It also creates a major risk in that popular resentment against the regimes and their Western backers may cause their overthrow and the emergence of new anti-Western regimes. The 1979 Iranian revolution and the central involvement of Saudi citizens in the September 2001 terrorist attacks provide the sharpest examples of where this can lead, but Western defence diplomacy cooperation with authoritarian allies also contributes to more general anti-Western sentiment, especially in the Middle East. To the extent that democracy provides the best basis for long-term stability and security both within and between states, defence diplomacy cooperation with authoritarian regimes also undermines the longer-term prospects for the emergence of a more secure world. Given the competing interests shaping their foreign policies, Western governments are likely to continue to face a difficult balancing act between the perceived need for defence diplomacy cooperation with unsavoury allies and the longer-term benefits of promoting democracy and human rights.

A third pattern of defence diplomacy involves support to states undergoing major domestic change, in particular as a consequence of democratisation and/or post-conflict peace-building. This group encompasses a diverse range of countries in post-communist Europe, Africa, South America and Asia. In these states, the aim of Western defence diplomacy has been to support efforts to establish new national security policies and reform armed forces and security sectors, in particular by helping states to establish effective democratically based security forces and develop the capacity to deal with their own national and regional security problems. The prospects for successful defence diplomacy engagement in transitional states depend in significant part on the nature and difficulty of their transitions, which vary greatly. The relatively smooth democratic transitions of the Central and Eastern European states provided a receptive context for Western assistance in reforming civil–military relations. Indeed, these countries are now becoming part of the larger Western community of established democracies, and patterns of defence diplomacy with them are likely to converge with those among the more long-standing Western allies. In contrast, countries in other parts of the world have faced more difficult transitions. In Africa, there is an enormous gap between the current realities of African armed forces and the long-term goal of democratically controlled militaries capable of providing for national security and contributing to regional security. The ability of external defence diplomacy assistance to bridge that gap is inevitably limited. Some states, such as Nigeria and Indonesia, are characterised by partial or stalled transitions, where elements of democratisation are in place, but the military remains sufficiently powerful to resist further change. In these circumstances, external defence diplomacy engagement may be helpful, but achieving decisive breakthroughs is likely to be difficult. In other cases, such as Afghanistan, Bosnia and Sierra Leone, the effective use of defence diplomacy to support the development of new national armed forces is likely to be dependent on the establishment of an effectively functioning state. The nature, extent and prospects of defence diplomacy engagement with transitional states are therefore likely to vary greatly.

A fourth pattern of defence diplomacy interaction involves strategic engagement with former or potential enemies in order to prevent conflict with these states and improve wider political relations. At the global level, Western defence diplomacy towards Russia and China is the primary example of such engagement. At the regional level, various states have sought to use defence diplomacy in a similar way, and Western governments have encouraged multilateral military cooperation through frameworks such as the PfP and the ARF in order to help prevent conflicts amongst the states concerned. In future, if countries such as Iran and North Korea can be persuaded to abandon their nuclear weapon ambitions and reform, they might also be partners for such engagement. The use of defence diplomacy for purposes of strategic engagement and conflict prevention is in significant part dependent on the wider political context of the relationship concerned, and should be viewed as a long-term process.

These various types of relationship have also produced distinctive regional patterns of defence diplomacy. In Europe, the various goals of Western defence diplomacy were compatible and mutually reinforcing. NATO and the EU provided a strong political and institutional core around which defence diplomacy was built, Central and Eastern European states were willing partners and the prospect of NATO and EU membership provided a powerful incentive for states to implement reform. In other regions, the shift from old to new defence diplomacy has been less far-reaching, the strategic context has been less amenable and the tensions between new and old defence diplomacy have been clearer. In Asia, the US has sought to use new-style defence diplomacy to engage China, but this has been counterbalanced by parallel efforts to contain Beijing. While the ARF has to some extent become a forum for multilateral defence diplomacy, many of its members also remain averse to military transparency and wary of external involvement in their defence policies. In the Americas, new defence diplomacy goals have been advanced, but the US-led 'war on drugs' has taken precedence over, and to some extent undermined, these aims. In Africa, Western governments have advanced the new defence diplomacy goals of conflict prevention, democracy and enhancing regional peacekeeping capabilities, but achieving these aims is extremely challenging and African states are suspicious of Western intentions. In the Middle East, patterns of military cooperation continue to be shaped almost entirely by old defence diplomacy goals. How far the overthrow of Saddam Hussein in Iraq will alter this – for example, by resulting in new policies to engage Iraq and Iran or stronger external pressure for democratisation in the region – remains to be seen.

Defence diplomacy also involves a number of policy challenges, dilemmas and trade-offs for Western governments. The expansion of defence diplomacy and its use to pursue new goals is itself contentious. Some critics argue that the new defence diplomacy's focus on cooperation and 'soft' dimensions of military activity make it naive and unrealistic, at best delusional and, in the worst case, undermining the ability of armed forces to perform core war-fighting functions and transferring vital technical know-how and capabilities to future enemies. Other critics argue that the expansion of defence diplomacy gives undue influence to the military over foreign policymaking, militarises foreign policy and reinforces a long tradition of military cooperation with authoritarian regimes and human-rights abusers. While there are elements of truth in these criticisms, they also exaggerate the problems. There is no strong evidence to suggest that engagement in defence diplomacy has undermined the combat effectiveness of Western militaries. The risks of transferring dangerous know-how and capabilities to potential enemies are limited and can be managed. Whatever their merits, Western governments' military ties with authoritarian regimes have been and remain the result of decisions by democratically elected leaders, not the consequence of excessive influence from the military. To the extent that defence diplomacy can contribute to the development of cooperative relations with potential enemies such as Russia and China, help to prevent conflicts in various regions of the world, promote democratic civil–military relations and enhance other states' peacekeeping capabilities, it contributes in a very direct way to international security.

Western governments are likely to continue to use defence diplomacy as a means of strengthening allies against potential threats: the new NATO members vis-a-vis Russia; Japan, Taiwan and other East Asian states vis-a-vis China; South Korea vis-a-vis North Korea; the Persian Gulf states vis-a-vis Iran; and various allies in the war against terrorism. At the same time, Western governments are also likely to continue defence diplomacy efforts to engage countries such as Russia and China. Achieving the right balance between these competing aims is a difficult and ongoing task.

Defence diplomacy should also be viewed as a long-term policy instrument that may only reap dividends after many years, even decades. Armed forces are large, complex organisations with entrenched cultures. Overcoming decades of Cold War mistrust on the part of the Russian and Chinese militaries will take a great deal of time and effort. Consolidating democratic civilian control of armed forces and developing the capabilities necessary to contribute to peacekeeping operations require major changes in armed forces' organisation, culture, training and equipment. Generational change will be particularly important, and the full benefits of defence diplomacy may not be seen until new generations of officers move up through the ranks. Western governments therefore need to have patience when defence diplomacy does not produce dramatic results overnight, and provide sustained long-term support for engagement with other countries, even when there are setbacks in the reform process.

Issues of democracy and human rights are likely to continue to pose central dilemmas for the use of defence diplomacy. This reflects two more general tensions in Western foreign and security policies. First, there are tensions between the long-term goal of promoting democracy and human rights and more narrow strategic or economic interests, with the latter sometimes leading Western governments to support authoritarian allies. Second, there are tensions between the logic of engagement, which suggests that cooperation should be pursued in order to encourage reform even if partners' records on democracy and human rights may be poor, and the logic of conditionality, which suggests that cooperation should be conditional on reform. Neither of these tensions is likely to be easily resolved. Thus, while democracy and the promotion of democratic civil–military relations and respect for human rights have assumed much greater prominence in Western defence diplomacy, there are also likely to be continuing pressures to support authoritarian allies of convenience in various situations – despite the risks. Although the September 2001 attacks have led to a shift back towards the old defence diplomacy of supporting allies despite their authoritarianism, there are also countervailing pressures to give greater primacy to democracy promotion, and it remains to be seen how far this shift will go.

Defence diplomacy also relates to wider issues of international burden-sharing, cooperation and division of labour. Given America's status as the world's only superpower and its global military predominance, the US not surprisingly plays the leading role in international defence diplomacy. Other states, however, also contribute significantly: countries such as Britain, Germany and non-NATO member Sweden are important participants in defence diplomacy in Central and Eastern Europe; Britain and France are playing a leading role in efforts to promote military reform in Africa; and ASEAN states have been the driving force behind efforts to promote multilateral security cooperation in East Asia. Nevertheless, there is a danger that America's leading role may contribute to a number of negative tendencies: US resentment at a perceived lack of burden-sharing, creating pressures to disengage from defence diplomacy activities; perceptions that defence diplomacy is simply a US rather than a wider international activity, undermining its legitimacy; and divisions between the US and its allies, which may be exploited by other states. Given these dangers, Western Europe, Australia, Japan and South Korea need to consider how they can contribute more to defence diplomacy efforts, and perhaps add value through the development of niche expertise. Western Europe, for example, has a strong interest in, and should contribute more to, Russian military reform. Japan, South Korea and Australia, as well as European states, could contribute more to military engagement with China. Greater defence engagement by non-regional states in South America could help to counterbalance concerns about US predominance and provide examples of other models of democratically controlled militaries. Given the EU's growing engagement with all regions of the world and its emerging – albeit so far limited – military role, the Union should also explore whether it can contribute more collectively to defence diplomacy as an external policy instrument.

Despite the expansion of defence diplomacy activities over the last decade, there has been little comparative analysis of such activities and there have been few attempts to evaluate the effectiveness of military cooperation and assistance. Despite numerous efforts to rebuild armed forces in previously war-torn states and to help democratising states reform their militaries, when it became clear in late 2001 that Afghanistan was in urgent need of support there was no collective international repository of knowledge on how similar challenges had been addressed elsewhere. Similarly, although Western states have been seeking to support the democratisation of civil–military relations in Africa, Central and Eastern Europe and South America, these projects have remained largely separate and there has been little comparative analysis of the challenges involved and the effectiveness of different forms of assistance. Western governments can and should do more to establish formal procedures and mechanisms for evaluating the effectiveness of defence diplomacy activities, and should undertake more comparative analysis of the lessons to be learned from experiences in different regions and countries.

The concept of defence diplomacy encapsulates the idea that armed forces and related defence infrastructures have the potential to contribute to international security, not only by deterring and if necessary fighting wars, but also by helping to promote a more cooperative and stable international environment. Defence diplomacy is not an alternative to the more traditional roles of armed forces or to other foreign and security policy instruments, but rather a supplement to them. In the contemporary strategic environment – with Russia and the West attempting to build a post-confrontation relationship, China and the US torn between cooperation and competition, many countries around the world attempting to consolidate democracy and overcome internal conflicts and the West seeking to disrupt international terrorist groups and address the conditions that help give rise to terrorism – defence diplomacy has the potential to make an important contribution to the long-term development of a more cooperative and stable international order. The challenge for governments is to creatively exploit this potential.

Notes

Acknowledgements

This paper draws on a project on
the Transformation of Civil-Military
Relations in Comparative Context,
funded by the Economic and Social
Research Council (ESRC) 'One
Europe or Several?' Programme
(award number L213252009). The
UK Ministry of Defence also
provided support for the
researching of this paper. The
authors would like to thank
Professor Edward C. Page, Director
of the ESRC's 'Future Governance'
Programme and Stephen Pollard
and Malcolm Howarth from the UK
Ministry of Defence who sponsored
a workshop on Defence Diplomacy
in Comparative Perspective in 2001.
The authors wish to thank Mats
Berdal, Malcolm Chalmers, Tim
Edmunds, Tim Huxley, Charles
Moskos, David Shambaugh, Peter
Viggo Jakobsen and John Allen
Williams for their comments on this
paper. The contents are entirely the
responsibility of the authors.

Introduction

1   E. S. Williams, *Cold War, Hot Seat:
    A Western Defence Attaché in the
    Soviet Union* (London: Robert
    Hale: 2000), pp. 20–21.
2   'Partnership for Peace: Framework
    Document', *NATO Review*, vol. 42,
no. 1, February 1994, pp. 29–30.
3   William S. Cohen, US Secretary of
    Defense, *Report of the Quadrennial
    Defense Review* (Washington DC:
    Department of Defense, May 1997),
    http://defenselink.mil/pubs/qdr;
    and Ashton B. Carter and William
    J. Perry, *Preventive Defense: A New
    Security Strategy for America*
    (Washington DC: Brookings
    Institution Press, 1999).
4   The defence diplomacy mission is
    defined as 'To provide forces to
    meet the varied activities
    undertaken by the Ministry of
    Defence to dispel hostility, build
    and maintain trust and assist in
    the development of democratically
    accountable armed forces, thereby
    making a significant contribution
    to conflict prevention and
    resolution'. Ministry of Defence,
    Defence Diplomacy, Paper 1
    (London: Ministry of Defence,
    2000), p. 2.
5   Arms control, non-proliferation
    and confidence-building do not fit
    within the definition of defence
    diplomacy used in this paper.
    Arms control is probably better
    understood as a distinct activity in
    its own right, rather than as a sub-
    component of defence diplomacy.

Chapter 1

1   Speech by Secretary of State for

Defence George Robertson, 'NATO for a New Generation', Atlantic Council (UK), 19 November 1997, UK Ministry of Defence website, www.mod.uk/index.php3?page=43&nid=2466&CAT=33&VIEW=492.

2   For a critical assessment of the impact of Australia's defence engagement with Indonesia see Don Greenless, 'Khaki Diplomacy Under Post-Timor Constraints', The Australian, 10 March 2000, www.etan.org/et2000a/march/5-11/10khaki.htm.

3   The first meeting of a US Secretary of Defense (Frank Carlucci) and his Soviet counterpart (General Staff Chief Sergei Akhromeyev) took place in 1987. A two-year programme of US–Soviet military contacts was agreed in 1989. See Marybeth Peterson Ulrich, *Democratizing Communist Militaries: The Case of the Czech and Russian Armed Forces* (Ann Arbor, MI: The University of Michigan Press, 1999), p. 52.

4   'Major Milestones in NATO–Russia Relations: A Chronology of Important Events', NATO website, www.nato.int/docu/basictxt/fndact-c.htm; Douglas L. Clarke, 'Uncomfortable Partners', *Transition*, 15 February 1995, pp. 27–31; and Founding Act on Mutual Relations, Cooperation and Security between NATO and the Russian Federation, Paris, 27 May 1997, NATO website, www.nato.int/docu/basictxt/fndact-a.htm.

5   Author's discussions with NATO officials, NATO headquarters, Brussels, 1999.

6   Peterson Ulrich, *Democratizing Communist Militaries*, pp. 165–66.

7   See Dale Herspring, 'De-Professionalising the Russian Armed Forces', in Anthony Forster et al., *The Challenge of Military Reform in Postcommunist Europe: Building Professional Armed Forces* (Houndmills: Palgrave, 2002), pp. 197–210.

8   Ian Traynor, 'Russia Raises Nuclear Threat', *The Guardian*, 14 January 2000.

9   Alexander A. Belkin and James H. Brusstar, 'A Military in Charge of Itself: Civilian Control Is a Russian Myth', *Strategic Forum*, no. 59 (Washington DC: National Defense University, Institute for National Strategic Studies, October 1995); and Irina Isakova, 'The Evolution of Civil–Military Relations in Russia', in Andrew Cottey et al., *Democratic Control of the Military in Postcommunist Europe: Guarding the Guards* (Houndmills: Palgrave, 2001), pp. 215–32.

10   Dmitri Trenin, 'Russia–NATO Relations: Time To Pick Up the Pieces', *NATO Review*, vol. 48, no. 1, Spring/Summer 2000, p. 21 (emphasis in original).

11   'Under Secretary Feith Joint Media Availability with Russian First Deputy Chief', News Transcript, 16 January 2002, US Department of Defense website, www.defenselink.mil/news/Jan2002/t01162002_t0116fba.html.

12   'Special Briefing on the Russian Visit', News Transcript, 16 January 2002, US Department of Defense website, www.defenselink.mil/news/Jan2002/t01162002_t0116fb.html.

13   See 'The Ebb and Flow of US–China Military Exchanges', in David Shambaugh, *Modernizing China's Military: Progress, Problems, and Prospects* (Berkeley, CA and London: University of California Press, 2002); and David Shambaugh, *Enhancing Sino-American Military Relations*, Sigur Center Asia Paper 4 (Washington DC: Sigur Center for Asian Studies, 1998).

14   'Background Note: China, Bureau of East Asian and Pacific Affairs', January 2002, US Department of State website, www.state.gov/r/pa/bgn/2742.h

tm; and Carter and Perry, *Preventive Defense*, p. 93.

[15] David Shambaugh, 'Sino-American Strategic Relations: From Partners to Competitors', *Survival*, vol. 42, no. 1, Spring 2000, p. 113, fn. 1.

[16] Carter and Perry, *Preventive Defense*, pp. 94–95 and 100.

[17] Shambaugh, 'Sino-American Strategic Relations', pp. 101, 107 and 114, fn. 10.

[18] Shambaugh, *Modernizing China's Military*; and James A Kelly, Assistant Secretary of State for East Asian and Pacific Affairs, 'The Future of US–China Relations', Testimony before the Senate Foreign Relations Committee, Subcommittee on East Asian and Pacific Affairs, Washington DC, 1 May 2001, US Department of State website, www.state.gov/r/eap/rls/r/2001/2697.htm.

[19] 'A Hint of the Cold War over the South China Sea', *The Economist*, 7 April 2001, pp. 65–66.

[20] US–China Inter-Agency Partnership to Fight Terrorism, Ambassador Francis X. Taylor, Remarks to the Press, Beijing, China, 6 December 2001, US Department of State website, www.state.gov/s/ct/rls/2001/6689.htm.

[21] *The United States Security Strategy for the East Asia-Pacific Region 1998* (Washington DC: Department of Defense, 1998), www.defenselink.mil/pubs/easr98/easr98.pdf, pp. 6, 30–34 and 64–65; 'Military-to-Military Exchanges with the People's Liberation Army', Deputy Secretary of Defense, Washington DC, 8 June 2001, www.defenselink.mil/news/Jun2001/d20010626m2m.pdf; Shambaugh, 'Sino-American Strategic Relations', pp. 107–109; and Carter and Perry, *Preventive Defense*, pp. 107 and 109.

[22] *Ibid.*, p. 100.

[23] Shambaugh, 'Sino-American Strategic Relations', pp. 107 and 110.

Chapter 2

[1] Both the Clinton and Bush administrations made support for democracy a central element of their national security strategies. See *A National Security Strategy of Engagement and Enlargement* (Washington DC: The White House, February 1995); and *The National Security Strategy of the United States of America* (Washington DC: The White House, September 2002), www.whitehouse.gov/nsc/nss.html.

[2] Samuel P. Huntington, *The Third Wave: Democratization in the Late Twentieth Century* (Norman, OK and London: University of Oklahoma Press, 1991).

[3] Although the democratic peace hypothesis remains controversial, and unstable, democratising states may actually increase the likelihood of conflict, there is substantial evidence to support the argument that stable, established democracies do not go to war with one another. See Bruce Russett, *Grasping the Democratic Peace: Principles for a Post-Cold War World* (Princeton, NJ: Princeton University Press, 1993).

[4] This logic was explicitly adopted by the Clinton administration. See *A National Security Strategy of Engagement and Enlargement*, p. 2 and pp. 22–24.

[5] The preamble to the 1949 North Atlantic Treaty commits NATO's members to 'safeguard the freedom, common heritage and civilisation of their peoples, founded on the principles of democracy, individual liberty and the rule of law'. *The North Atlantic Treaty*, Washington DC, 4 April 1949.

6   The promotion of democratic civil–military relations in post-communist Europe was identified as a goal from the early 1990s onwards. See 'North Atlantic Cooperation Council Statement on Dialogue Partnership and Cooperation, 20 December 1991', *NATO Review*, vol. 40, no. 1, February 1992, p. 30; and 'Statement Issued at the Meeting of Defence Ministers at NATO Headquarters, Brussels, 1 April 1992', *ibid.*, vol. 40, no. 2, April 1992, pp. 32–33.

7   Partnership for Peace Framework Document (10–11 January 1994), *ibid.*, vol. 42, no. 1, February 1994, p. 29.

8   Membership Action Plan (MAP), issued at the meeting of the North Atlantic Council in Washington DC, 23–24 April 1999, *ibid.*, vol. 47, no. 2, Summer 1999, p. D14.

9   This section draws on Andrew Cottey et al, *Democratic Control of the Military in Postcommunist Europe.*

10 Thomas S. Szayna, *The Military in a Postcommunist Poland*, N-2209-USDP (Santa Monica, CA: RAND, 1991), p. 43.

11 Alex J. Bellamy, 'A Revolution in Civil–Military Affairs: The Professionalisation of Croatia's Armed Forces', in Anthony Forster et al, *The Challenge of Military Reform in Postcommunist Europe*, pp. 165–82; and Jonathan Steele, 'Croatia's President Gives Seven Generals Their Marching Orders', *The Guardian*, 30 September 2000.

12 Alice Lagnando, 'US Courts Uzbekistan Despite Rights Abuse', *The Times*, 10 August 2002, p. 15.

13 *Ibid.*; and Pauline Jones Luong and Erika Weinthal, 'New Friends, New Fears in Central Asia', *Foreign Affairs*, March–April 2002 vol. 81, no. 2.

14 Abraham F. Lowenthal (ed.), *Armies and Politics in Latin America* (New York and London: Holmes and Meier Publishers Inc., 1976).

15 Jenny Pearce, *Under the Eagle: US Intervention in Central America and the Caribbean* (London: America Bureau, 1982); and Lars Schoultz, *Beneath the United States: A History of US Policy Toward Latin America* (Cambridge, MA: Harvard University Press, 1998).

16 Andrew Hurrell, 'The United States and Latin America: Neorealism Re-examined', in Ngaire Woods (ed.), *Explaining International Relations Since 1945* (Oxford: Oxford University Press, 1996), p. 175.

17 *United States Security Strategy for the Americas* (Washington DC: Department of Defense, Office of International Security Affairs, September 1995), p. 21.

18 Adam Isacson and Joy Olson, *Just the Facts: A Civilian's Guide to US Defense and Security Assistance to Latin America and the Caribbean* (Washington DC: Latin America Working Group in cooperation with the Centre for International Policy, November 2001).

19 'Foreign Military Interaction', *ibid.*

20 Lars Schoultz, *National Security and United States Policy Toward Latin America* (Princeton, NJ: Princeton University Press, 1987), pp. 181–82.

21 Ambler H. Moss, Jr., 'A New Vision of US–Latin American Relations' and Donald E. Schulz, 'The Role of the US Army in Promoting Democracy in the Americas', in Max G. Manwaring (ed.), *Security and Civil–Military Relations in the New World Disorder: The Use of Armed Forces in the Americas* (Carlisle, PA: US Army War College Strategic Studies Institute, September 1999), pp. 35–48.

22 See 'Training: Findings and Recommendations', in Adam Isacson and Joy Olson, *Just the Facts 2000–2001: A Quick Tour of US Defense and Security Relations*

with Latin America and the Caribbean (Washington DC: Latin America Working Group in cooperation with the Center for International Policy, November 2001), www.ciponline.org/facts/traifdin.htm.

23 *United States Security Strategy for the Americas*, pp. 22–23; and 'E-IMET: Expanded International Military Training and Education', in Isacson and Olson, *Just the Facts: A Civilian's Guide to US Defense and Security Assistance to Latin America and the Caribbean*.

24 John T. Fishel and Kimbra L. Fishel, 'The Impact of the US Army School of the Americas on Host Nation Militaries: An Effective Instrument of Policy or Merely a Scapegoat', *Low Intensity Conflict & Law Enforcement*, vol. 7, no. 1, Summer 1998, pp. 47–70; *United States Security Strategy for the Americas*, p. 23; John A. Cope, *International Military Training and Assistance: An Assessment*, McNair Paper 44 (Washington DC: Institute for National Strategic Studies, National Defense University, October 1995), pp. 21–23; and 'School of the Americas (Western Hemisphere Institute for Security Cooperation)', in Isacson and Olson, *Just the Facts*, www.ciponline.org/facts/soa.htm

25 'Centre for Hemispheric Defense Studies', *ibid.*, www.ciponline.org/facts/chds.htm.

26 'Foreign Military Interaction', *ibid.*, www.ciponline.org/facts/fmi.htm

27 Isacson and Olson, *Just the Facts*, www.ciponline.org/facts.

28 Russell Crandell, 'Clinton, Bush and Plan Colombia', *Survival*, vol. 44, no. 1, Spring 2002, pp. 159–72.

29 Doug Stokes, 'Why the end of the Cold War doesn't matter: the US war of terror in Colombia', *Review of International Studies*, vol. 29 no. 4, October 2003, pp. 569–586, p. 571.

30 Julian Borger and Alex Bellos, 'US "Gave the Nod" to Venezuelan Coup', *The Guardian*, 17 April 2002; Duncan Campbell, 'American Navy "Helped Venezuelan Coup"', *ibid.*, 29 April 2002; and Greg Palast, 'Opec Chief Warned Chavez about Coup', *ibid.*, 13 May 2002.

31 On divisions within the US government regarding policy towards Venezuela, see Andy Webb-Vidal, 'US Envoy Revokes Visa of Former General', *Financial Times*, 13 June 2003.

Chapter 3

1 'Partnership for Peace: Framework Document', p. 29.

2 Meeting of the North Atlantic Cooperation Council, Athens, Greece, 11 June 1993, Report to Ministers by the NACC Ad Hoc Group on Cooperation in Peacekeeping, *NATO Review*, vol. 41, no. 4, August 1993, pp. 30–35; and Meeting of the North Atlantic Cooperation Council, NATO Headquarters, Brussels, 3 December 1993, Report to Ministers by the NACC Ad Hoc Group on Cooperation in Peacekeeping, *ibid.*, vol. 41, no. 6, December 1993, pp. 27–30.

3 'PfP Training Exercises Get Under Way', *ibid.*, vol. 42, no. 5, October 1994, p. 24.

4 Washington Summit Communique, Issued by the Heads of State and Government participating in the meeting of the North Atlantic Council in Washington, DC, on 24 April 1999, Press Release NAC-S-(99)64, 24 April 1999.

5 *Allied Approaches to Defence Diplomacy*, Defence Diplomacy Study Report 3, Centre for Defence Studies, King's College London, June 2001.

6 For a detailed discussion of the role of the WEU and the EU in defence outreach with the countries of Central and Eastern

Europe, see Andrew Cottey, 'The European Dimension of Defense Reform: From the WEU to the EU's New Defense Role', chapter 2 in Istvan Gyarmati and Theodor Winkler, eds., *Post-Cold War Defense Reforms: Lessons Learned in Europe and the United States*, (Washington, DC: Brassey's, 2002), pp. 19–35.

7 Pal Dunay, 'Building Professional Competence in Hungary's Defence: Slow Motion', in Forster et al., (eds), *The Challenge of Military Reform in Postcommunist Europe*, p. 67.

8 Darren Lake, 'Shape of Security Force Causes Controversy', *Jane's Defence Weekly*, 16 January 2002.

9 For a detailed discussion of this process, see Forster et al, *The Challenge of Military Reform in Postcommunist Europe.*

10 Agence France-Presse, 'Baltics Must Rethink Defense Strategies, Conscription: Latvian Defmin', *NATO Enlargement Daily Brief* (NEDB), 17 January 2003.

11 Association of Concerned African Scholars, *US Military Programs in Sub-Saharan Africa, 2001–2003*, www.prairienet.org/acas/military /miloverview.html.

12 'Trying on blue berets', *The Economist*, 11 September 2003.

13 Justin Morris and Hilaire McCoubrey, 'Regional Peacekeeping in the Post-Cold War Era', *International Peacekeeping*, vol. 6, no. 2, pp. 129–51.

14 Eric G. Berman and Katie E. Sams, *Constructive Disengagement: Western Efforts to Develop African Peacekeeping*, Monograph 33 (Pretoria: Institute for Security Studies, December 1998), www.iss.co.za/Pubs/Monograph s/No33/Capacity.html.

15 *Ibid.*

16 Eric Berman and Katie Sams, *Peacekeeping in Africa: Capabilities and Culpabilities* (Geneva: UNIDIR, March 2000).

17 The members of ECOWAS are:

Benin, Burkina Faso, Cape Verde, Côte d'Ivoire, Gambia, Ghana, Guinea, Guinea-Bissau, Liberia, Mali, Niger, Nigeria, Senegal, Sierra Leone and Togo. See Peter Viggo Jakobsen, 'UN Peace Operations', in Boris Knodoch (ed.), *International Peacekeeping Yearbook 2001* (The Hague: Kluwer Press International, 2001), pp. 151–78.

18 W. D. Bajusz and K. P. O'Prey, 'An All African Peace Force: An Immediate Option or Long Term Goal for the Region?', *Strategic Forum*, no. 86, October 1996, www.ndu.edu/inss/strforum/SF _86/forum86.html.

19 Berman and Sams, *Constructive Disengagement*; and William Nhara, 'Conflict Management and Peace Operations: The Role of the Organisation of African Unity and Subregional Organisations', in Mark Malan (ed.), *Resolute Partners: Building Peacekeeping Capacity in Southern Africa*, Monograph 21 (Pretoria: Institute for Security Studies, February 1998), www.iss.co.za/Pubs/Monographs /No21/Nhara.html.

20 David O'Brien, 'The Search for Subsidiarity: The UN, African Regional Organisations and Humanitrian Action', *International Peacekeeping*, vol. 7, no. 3, Autumn 2000, p. 65.

21 James Jamerson, 'A United States Contribution to Capacity-Building: The African Crisis Response Initiative', in Malan (ed.), *Resolute Partners.*

22 Berman and Sams, *Constructive Disengagement.*

23 Chris Smith, 'Security-sector Reform: Development Breakthrough or Institutional Engineering?', *Conflict, Security and Development*, vol. 1, no. 1, 2001, p. 11.

24 'How to put the house in order', *The Economist*, 13 March 2004, p. 48.